W9-ARQ-228

Full Color Every Page!

PC Upgrade & Repair
Simplified™

IDG's **3-D Visual™** Series

IDG BOOKS

From
maranGraphics™

IDG Books Worldwide, Inc.
An International Data Group Company
Foster City, CA • Indianapolis • Chicago • Southlake, TX

PC Upgrade & Repair Simplified™

Published by
IDG Books Worldwide, Inc.
An International Data Group Company
919 E. Hillsdale Blvd., Suite 400
Foster City, CA 94404
(650) 655-3000

Library of Congress Catalog Card No.: 98-072810

ISBN: 0-7645-6049-2

Printed in the United States of America

10 9 8 7 6 5 4 3 2 1

Distributed in the United States by IDG Books Worldwide, Inc.

Distributed by Transworld Publishers Limited in the United Kingdom; by IDG Norge Books for Norway; by IDG Sweden Books for Sweden; by Woodslane Pty. Ltd. for Australia; by Woodslane (NZ) Ltd. for New Zealand; by Addison Wesley Longman Singapore Pte Ltd. for Singapore, Malaysia, Thailand, Indonesia and Korea; by Norma Comunicaciones S.A. for Colombia; by Intersoft for South Africa; by International Thomson Publishing for Germany, Austria and Switzerland; by Toppan Company Ltd. for Japan; by Distribuidora Cuspide for Argentina; by Livraria Cultura for Brazil; by Ediciencia S.A. for Ecuador; by Ediciones ZETA S.C.R. Ltda. for Peru; by WS Computer Publishing Corporation, Inc., for the Philippines; by Unalis Corporation for Taiwan; by Contemporanea de Ediciones for Venezuela; by Computer Book & Magazine Store for Puerto Rico; by Express Computer Distributors for the Caribbean and West Indies. Authorized Sales Agent: Anthony Rudkin Associates for the Middle East and North Africa.
For corporate orders, please call maranGraphics at 800-469-6616.
For general information on IDG Books Worldwide's books in the U.S., please call our Consumer Customer Service department at 800-762-2974.
For reseller information, including discounts and premium sales, please call our Reseller Customer Service department at 800-434-3422.
For information on where to purchase IDG Books Worldwide's books outside the U.S., please contact our International Sales department at 650-655-3200 or fax 650-655-3297.
For information on foreign language translations, please contact our Foreign & Subsidiary Rights department at 650-655-3021 or fax 650-655-3281.
For sales inquiries and special prices for bulk quantities, please contact our Sales department at 650-655-3200.
For information on using IDG Books Worldwide's books in the classroom or for ordering examination copies, please contact our Educational Sales department at 800-434-2086 or fax 317-596-5499.
For press review copies, author interviews, or other publicity information, please contact our Public Relations department at 650-655-3000 or fax 650-655-3299.
For authorization to photocopy items for corporate, personal, or educational use, please contact maranGraphics at 800-469-6616.

Trademark Acknowledgments

©1998 maranGraphics, Inc.

The 3-D illustrations are the
copyright of maranGraphics, Inc.

U.S. Corporate Sales	**U.S. Trade Sales**
Contact maranGraphics at (800) 469-6616 or Fax (905) 890-9434.	Contact IDG Books at (800) 434-3422 or (650) 655-3000.

Welcome to the world of IDG Books Worldwide.

IDG Books Worldwide, Inc., is a subsidiary of International Data Group, the world's largest publisher of computer-related information and the leading global provider of information services on information technology. IDG was founded more than 25 years ago and now employs more than 8,500 people worldwide. IDG publishes more than 270 computer publications in over 75 countries (see listing below). More than 90 million people read one or more IDG publications each month.

Launched in 1990, IDG Books Worldwide is today the #1 publisher of best-selling computer books in the United States. We are proud to have received eight awards from the Computer Press Association in recognition of editorial excellence and three from Computer Currents' First Annual Readers' Choice Awards. Our best-selling ...For Dummies® series has more than 25 million copies in print with translations in 30 languages. IDG Books Worldwide, through a joint venture with IDG's Hi-Tech Beijing, became the first U.S. publisher to publish a computer book in the People's Republic of China. In record time, IDG Books Worldwide has become the first choice for millions of readers around the world who want to learn how to better manage their businesses.

Our mission is simple: Every one of our books is designed to bring extra value and skill-building instructions to the reader. Our books are written by experts who understand and care about our readers. The knowledge base of our editorial staff comes from years of experience in publishing, education, and journalism - experience which we use to produce books for the '90s. In short, we care about books, so we attract the best people. We devote special attention to details such as audience, interior design, use of icons, and illustrations. And because we use an efficient process of authoring, editing, and desktop publishing our books electronically, we can spend more time ensuring superior content and spend less time on the technicalities of making books.

You can count on our commitment to deliver high-quality books at competitive prices on topics you want to read about. At IDG Books Worldwide, we continue in the IDG tradition of delivering quality for more than 25 years. You'll find no better book on a subject than one from IDG Books Worldwide.

John Kilcullen
President and CEO
IDG Books Worldwide, Inc.

IDG Books Worldwide, Inc., is a subsidiary of International Data Group, the world's largest publisher of computer-related information and the leading global provider of information services on information technology. International Data Group publishes over 276 computer publications in over 75 countries. Ninety million people read one or more International Data Group publications each month. International Data Group's publications include: Argentina: Annuario de Informatica, Computerworld Argentina, PC World Argentina; Australia: Australian Macworld, Client/Server Journal, Computer Living, Computerworld, Computerworld 100, Digital News, IT Casebook, Network World, On-line World Australia, PC World, Publishing Essentials, Reseller, WebMaster; Austria: Computerwelt Osterreich, Networks Austria, PC Tip; Belarus: PC World Belarus; Belgium: Data News; Brazil: Annuário de Informática, Computerworld Brazil, Connections, Super Game Power, Macworld, PC Player, PC World Brazil, Publish Brazil, Reseller News; Bulgaria: Computerworld Bulgaria, Networkworld/Bulgaria, PC & MacWorld Bulgaria; Canada: CIO Canada, Client/Server World, ComputerWorld Canada, InfoCanada, Network World Canada; Chile: Computerworld Chile, PC World Chile; Colombia: Computerworld Colombia, PC World Colombia; Costa Rica: PC World Centro America; The Czech and Slovak Republics: Computerworld Czechoslovakia, Elektronika Czechoslovakia, Macworld Czech Republic, PC World Czechoslovakia; Denmark: Communications World, Computerworld Danmark, Macworld Danmark, PC Privat Danmark, PC World Danmark, PC World Danmark Supplements, TECH World; Dominican Republic: PC World Republica Dominicana; Ecuador: PC World Ecuador; Egypt: Computerworld Middle East, PC World Middle East; El Salvador: PC World Centro America; Finland: MikroPC, Tietoverkko, Tietoviikko; France: Distributique, Golden, Hebdo-Distributique, Info PC, Le Guide du Monde Informatique, Le Monde Informatique, Reseaux & Telecoms; Germany: Computer Partner, Computerwoche, Computerwoche Extra, Computerwoche Focus, I/M Information Management, Macwelt, PC Welt; Greece: GamePro, Multimedia World; Guatemala: PC World Centro America; Honduras: PC World Centro America; Hong Kong: Computerworld Hong Kong, PCWorld Hong Kong, Publish in Asia; Hungary: ABCD CD-ROM, Computerworld Szamitastechnika, PC & Mac World Hungary, PC-X Magazine; Iceland: Tolvuheimur/PC World Island; India: Information Systems Computerworld, PC World India, Publish in Asia; Indonesia: InfoKomputer PC World, Komputek Computerworld, Publish in Asia; Ireland: ComputerScope, PC Live!; Israel: People & Computers; Italy: Computerworld Italia, Computerworld Italia Special Editions, Macworld Italia, Networking Italia, PC Shopping, PC World Italia, PC World/Walt Disney; Japan: DTP World, HP Open World Japan, Macworld Japan, Nikkei Personal Computing, Open World Japan, OS/2 World Japan, SunWorld Japan, Windows World Japan; Kenya: East African Computer News; Korea: Hi-Tech Information/Computerworld, Macworld Korea, PC World Korea; Macedonia: PC World Macedonia; Malaysia: Computerworld Malaysia, PC World Malaysia, Publish in Asia; Mexico: Computerworld Mexico, Macworld, PC World Mexico; Myanmar: PC World Myanmar; Netherlands: Computer! Totaal, LAN Magazine, LanWorld Buyers Guide, Macworld, Net Magazine, Totaal! Beurskrant; New Zealand: Absolute Beginner's Guide, Computer Buyer, Computer Industry Directory, Computerworld New Zealand, MTB, Network World, PC World New Zealand; Nicaragua: PC World Centro America; Nigeria: PC World Nigeria; Norway: Computerworld Norge, Computerworld Privat (Datamagasinet), CW Rapport Norge, IDG's KURSGUIDE, Macworld Norge, Multimediaworld, PC World Ekspress, PC World Nettverk, PC World Norge, PC World's Produktguide, Windows World Spesial; Pakistan: Computerworld Pakistan, PC World Pakistan; Panama: PC World Panama; P. R. of China: China Computer Users, China Computerworld, China Infoworld, China Telecom World Weekly, Computer & Communication, Electronic Design China, Electronics Today, Electronics Weekly, Game Camp, Game Soft, Network World China, PC World China, Popular Computer Weekly, Software Weekly, Software World, Telecom World; Peru: Computerworld Peru, PC World Profesional Peru, PC World Peru; Poland: Computerworld Poland, Computerworld Special Report, Macworld, Networld, PC World Komputer; Philippines: Computerworld Philippines, PC World Philippines, Publish in Asia; Portugal: Cerebro/PC World, Computerworld/Correio Informático, Dealer World Portugal, Mac*In/PC*In, Multimedia World Portugal; Puerto Rico: PC World Puerto Rico; Romania: Computerworld Romania, PC World Romania, Telecom Romania; Russia: Computerworld Russia, Mir PK, Sety; Singapore: Computerworld Singapore, PC World Singapore, Publish in Asia; Slovenia: MONITOR; South Africa: Computing S.A., InfoWorld S.A., Network World S.A., Software World; Spain: Computerworld Espa-a, COMUNICACIONES WORLD, Dealer World, Macworld Espa-a, PC World Espa-a; Sweden: CAP&Design, Computer Sweden, Corporate Computing, MacWorld, Maxi Data, MikroDatorn, Nätverk & Kommunikation, PC/Aktiv, PC World, Windows World; Switzerland: Computerworld Schweiz, Macworld Schweiz, PCtip; Taiwan: Computerworld Taiwan, Macworld Taiwan, PC World Taiwan, Publish Taiwan, Windows World; Thailand: Thai Computerworld, Publish in Asia; Turkey: Computerworld Turkiye, MACWORLD Turkiye, PC WORLD Turkiye; Ukraine: Computerworld Kiev, Computers & Software, Multimedia World Ukraine, PC World Ukraine; United Kingdom: Acorn User, Amiga Action, Amiga Computing, Appletalk, Computing, GamePro, Macworld, Network News, Parents and Computers, PC Advisor, PC Home, PSX Pro UK, The WEB; United States: Cable in the Classroom, CD Review, CIO Magazine, Computerworld, Computerworld Client/Server Journal, Digital Video Magazine, DOS World, Federal Computer Week, GamePro, InfoWorld, I-Way, JavaWorld, Macworld, Multimedia World, Netscape World Online, Network World, PC Entertainment, PC World, Publish, SunWorld Online, SWATPro Magazine, Video Event, WebMaster; Uruguay: PC World Uruguay; Venezuela: Computerworld Venezuela, PC World Venezuela; and Vietnam: PC World Vietnam.

*Every maranGraphics book represents
the extraordinary vision and commitment of a unique family:
the Maran family of Toronto, Canada.*

Back Row (from left to right): *Sherry Maran, Rob Maran, Richard Maran, Maxine Maran, Jill Maran.*
Front Row (from left to right): *Judy Maran, Ruth Maran.*

Richard Maran is the company founder and its inspirational leader. He developed maranGraphics' proprietary communication technology called "visual grammar." This book is built on that technology—empowering readers with the easiest and quickest way to learn about computers.

Ruth Maran is the Author and Architect—a role Richard established that now bears Ruth's distinctive touch. She creates the words and visual structure that are the basis for the books.

Judy Maran is the Project Manager. She works with Ruth, Richard and the highly talented maranGraphics illustrators, designers and editors to transform Ruth's material into its final form.

Rob Maran is the Technical and Production Specialist. He makes sure the state-of-the-art technology used to create these books always performs as it should.

Sherry Maran manages the Reception, Order Desk and any number of areas that require immediate attention and a helping hand.

Jill Maran is a jack-of-all-trades who works in the Accounting and Human Resources department.

Maxine Maran is the Business Manager and family sage. She maintains order in the business and family—and keeps everything running smoothly.

CREDITS

Author:
Paul Whitehead

Copy Development Directors:
Kelleigh Wing
Wanda Lawrie

Copy Developers:
Roxanne Van Damme
Jason M. Brown
Cathy Benn

Project Manager:
Judy Maran

Editors:
Raquel Scott
Janice Boyer
Michelle Kirchner
James Menzies
Frances LoPresti
Emmet Mellow

Layout Design & Illustrations:
Jamie Bell
Treena Lees

Illustrators:
Russ Marini
Jeff Jones
Peter Grecco

Indexer:
Raquel Scott

Permissions Coordinator:
Jenn Hillman

Post Production:
Robert Maran

Editorial Support:
Michael Roney

ACKNOWLEDGMENTS

Thanks to the dedicated staff of maranGraphics, including
Jamie Bell, Cathy Benn, Janice Boyer, Jason M. Brown,
Francisco Ferreira, Peter Grecco, Jenn Hillman, Sean Johannesen,
Jeff Jones, Michelle Kirchner, Wanda Lawrie, Treena Lees,
Frances LoPresti, Jill Maran, Judy Maran, Maxine Maran,
Robert Maran, Ruth Maran, Sherry Maran, Russ Marini,
Emmet Mellow, James Menzies, Steven Schaerer, Raquel Scott,
Roxanne Van Damme and Kelleigh Wing.

Finally, to Richard Maran who originated the easy-to-use
graphic format of this guide. Thank you for your inspiration
and guidance.

PERMISSIONS

Advanced Micro Devices

Copyright © 1998 Advanced Micro Devices, Inc.
Reprinted with permission of copyright owner.
All rights reserved.

AMD, the AMD logo, 3Dnow!, AMD-K6-2, AMD-K6-2 logo
are trademarks of Advanced Micro Devices, Inc. and
AMD-K6 is a registered trademark, and may not be used
in advertising or publicity pertaining to distribution of this
information without specific, written prior permission.

American Power Conversion

American Power Conversion © 1998

Cyrix

Cyrix is a registered trademark and M II and MediaGX are
trademarks of Cyrix Corporation, a subsidiary of National
Semiconductor Corporation.

Dell Computers

Dell is a registered trademark of Dell Computer Corporation.

ENERGY STAR

ENERGY STAR is a US registered mark.

Imation

Travan is a trademark of Imation Corp. SuperDisk,
the SuperDisk logo, and the compatibility symbol are
trademarks of Imation Corp.

Iomega

Copyright © 1998 Iomega Corporation. All rights reserved.
Iomega, Zip and Jaz are registered trademarks of Iomega
Corporation.

Microsoft

Screen shots reprinted with permission from
Microsoft Corporation.

Zenith

Zenith Electronics Corp.

**The following companies have also given us
permission to use their screen shots, chips, etc.:**

ATI Technology
Award Software
Belkin
3Com
Creative Labs
Expert Color
Fujitsu
Hewlett-Packard
Intel
Keytronic
Lab Tec
Panasonic
Quantum
Sunkist
SyQuest
Tatung
Toshiba

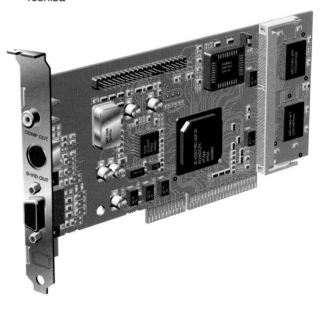

TABLE OF CONTENTS

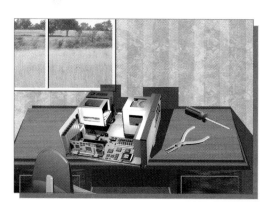

CHAPTER 3
INPUT AND OUTPUT DEVICES

CHAPTER 4
COMMUNICATION DEVICES

TABLE OF CONTENTS

CHAPTER 5
STORAGE DEVICES

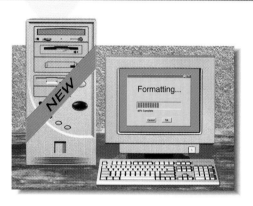

CHAPTER 6
MAINTAIN A COMPUTER

CHAPTER 7
UPGRADE A COMPUTER

CHAPTER 8
REPAIR A COMPUTER

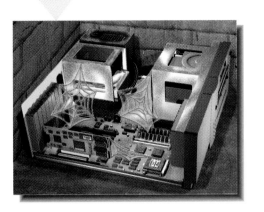

CHAPTER 9
PURCHASE A NEW COMPUTER

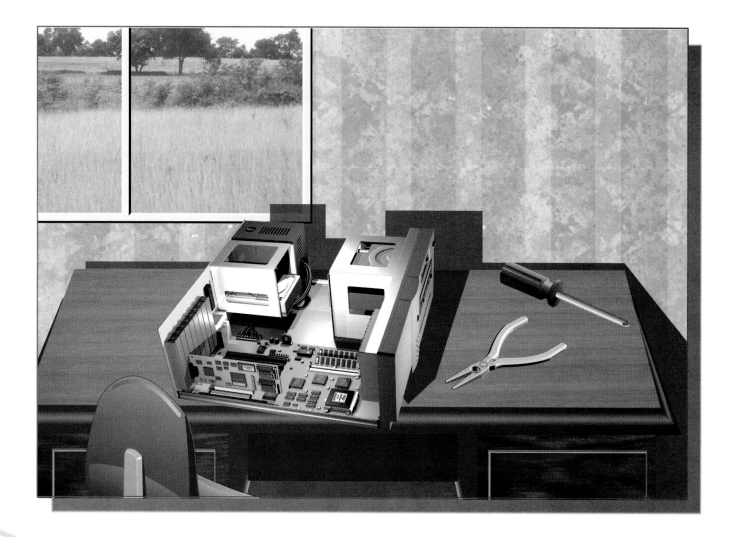

CHAPTER 1

UPGRADE AND REPAIR BASICS

There are many factors to consider when preparing to upgrade or repair your computer. This chapter discusses the tools you will need, how to protect components and connect devices and much more.

INTRODUCTION TO PC UPGRADE AND REPAIR SIMPLIFIED

WHO IS THIS BOOK FOR?

PC Upgrade and Repair Simplified is for anyone who wants to learn computer upgrade and repair techniques. Performing your own upgrades and repairs can save you money and increase your knowledge about computers and computer components.

INSTALL COMPONENTS AND DEVICES

PC Upgrade and Repair Simplified uses pictures to guide you step by step through installing internal components, such as an expansion card or a CPU. This book also uses pictures to show you how to connect external devices, such as a keyboard or scanner.

LEARN TO UPGRADE AND REPAIR

This book will teach you how to keep your computer up-to-date by upgrading components and devices. You will also learn how to determine the cause of common computer problems and how to repair those problems.

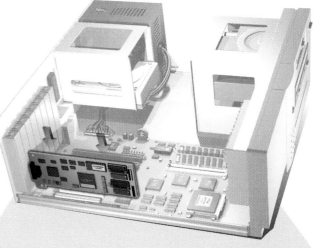

CONSIDERATIONS

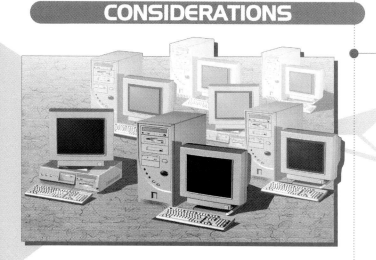

TYPE OF COMPUTER

You do not need a particular type of personal computer to complete the tasks shown in this book. *PC Upgrade and Repair Simplified* can help you upgrade and repair a wide variety of computer components and devices.

COMPUTER EXPERIENCE

You do not need any previous computer upgrade or repair experience to use *PC Upgrade and Repair Simplified*, but you should be familiar with the major components of the computer. You should also be familiar with the features and capabilities of your computer's operating system.

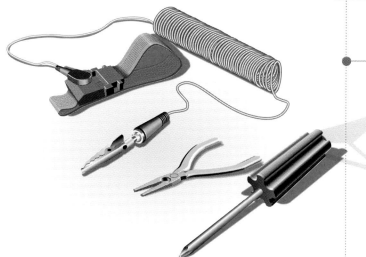

COMPUTER TOOLS

You can use common tools, such as a screwdriver, to perform most computer upgrades and repairs. Some tasks, however, may require you to use special tools, such as grounding devices. Grounding devices protect computer components from being damaged by static electricity. For information on computer tools, see page 6.

COMPUTER TOOLS

....

WHAT KIND OF TOOLS DO I NEED TO UPGRADE OR REPAIR MY COMPUTER SAFELY AND EFFICIENTLY?

There are several tools you can use. You can purchase a kit of commonly used computer tools at most computer stores.

SCREWDRIVER

You can use a slotted or Phillips screwdriver to insert and remove the screws on most computers. Some computers have screws that require a star-shaped screwdriver, called a torx driver.

You should not use an electric screwdriver when repairing a computer, since they tend to overtighten screws.

GROUNDING STRAP

Computer components can be damaged by static electricity. While repairing a computer, you should always wear a grounding strap to prevent the transfer of static electricity from your body to the computer. For information on protecting components from static electricity, see page 8.

PLIERS OR TWEEZERS

You can use a small set of pliers or sturdy pair of tweezers to adjust the jumpers on a system board or on a device such as a hard drive.

COMPRESSED AIR

You can use a can of compressed air to blow dust and dirt from inside a computer case. This can help make components easier to see and work with.

FLASHLIGHT

You can use a flashlight to illuminate the inside of a computer case. This can help make it easier to see components while repairing a computer.

MAGNET

Computer screws are very small and can often fall into hard-to-reach places inside the computer case. You can use a small magnet on the end of an extending rod to retrieve screws you have dropped.

CHIP REMOVER

A chip remover is a device you can use to remove a chip from its socket on a circuit board. A chip remover is often referred to as a chip extractor or chip puller.

PROTECT COMPONENTS FROM STATIC ELECTRICITY

WHY SHOULD I BE CONCERNED ABOUT STATIC ELECTRICITY WHEN UPGRADING OR REPAIRING MY COMPUTER?

Static electricity can damage computer components, especially those with complex circuits, such as a system board or CPU chip. When upgrading or repairing your computer, you must take precautions to protect the components.

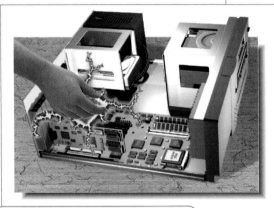

STATIC ELECTRICITY

Your body generates static electricity. Although you may not be able to detect the static electricity you generate, it is always present. You can transfer static electricity from your body to computer components just by touching them. ElectroStatic Discharge (ESD) is the term used to describe the transfer of static electricity from one object to another.

GROUNDING

When upgrading or repairing a computer, you should not touch the computer unless you and the computer are grounded. To ground yourself and the computer, you can use devices such as grounding wires, grounding straps and grounding mats.

GROUNDING DEVICES

Many grounding devices plug into the third hole on an electrical outlet. Grounding devices are available at most computer stores.

GROUNDING WIRE

You should always connect a metal part of the computer case to a grounding wire. When the computer case is grounded, you can touch a metal part of the computer case to ground yourself.

GROUNDING STRAP

You can wear a grounding strap on your wrist to prevent the transfer of static electricity from your body to computer components.

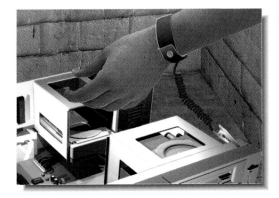

GROUNDING MAT

You can use a grounding mat to protect individual components from static electricity. You can position a grounding mat beside a computer and then place individual components on the mat.

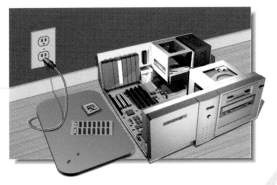

ANTI-STATIC BAGS

If you are removing a component from a computer for an extended period of time, you should store the component in an anti-static bag. Anti-static bags come in different sizes and are available at most computer stores.

CABLES AND CONNECTORS

HOW DO I CONNECT EXTERNAL AND INTERNAL DEVICES TO MY COMPUTER?

You can use cables and connectors to connect devices to your computer. Connectors with holes are called female connectors. Connectors with pins are called male connectors.

Most cables and connectors are unique and can connect only specific devices to a computer.

EXTERNAL CONNECTORS

Most external connectors are located at the back of the computer case. Some external connectors use screws or small clips to secure a connection.

KEYBOARD PORT

A keyboard port is a female connector with 6 holes, which allows you to connect a keyboard to the computer. This is known as a mini-DIN or PS/2 connector. Older computers have a larger keyboard port with 5 holes, known as a DIN connector.

MOUSE PORT

A mouse port is a female connector with 6 holes and is found on newer computers. Also known as a mini-DIN or PS/2 connector, a mouse port allows you to connect a mouse to the computer.

MONITOR PORT

A monitor port is a female connector with 15 holes. A monitor port allows you to use a monitor cable with a 15-pin male connector to connect a monitor to the computer.

PARALLEL PORT

A parallel port is a female connector with 25 holes. A parallel port allows you to use a parallel cable with a 25-pin male connector to connect a device such as a printer to the computer.

SERIAL PORT

A serial port can be a 9 or 25-pin male connector. A serial port allows you to use a serial cable with a 9 or 25-hole female connector to connect a device such as a mouse or external modem to the computer.

POWER CONNECTOR

A power connector is a 3-prong male connector. A power connector allows you to use a power cable with a 3-hole female connector to connect the computer to an electrical outlet on the wall.

EXTERNAL CONNECTORS continued

AUDIO JACK

Most computers have a sound card that contains several small, round audio jacks. Audio jacks allow you to connect devices such as speakers, headphones or a microphone to the computer.

JOYSTICK PORT

A joystick port is a female connector with 15 holes and is usually found on a sound card. A joystick port allows you to connect a joystick to the computer to play games. You can also use a joystick port to connect a musical instrument, such as an electronic synthesizer, to the computer.

MODEM JACK

A modem jack is the same type of connector as a telephone jack. A computer with an internal modem has two modem jacks. One jack allows you to plug a telephone line into the computer, while the other jack allows you to connect a telephone to the computer.

USB PORT

A Universal Serial Bus (USB) port is a small, rectangular connector that can support up to 127 devices, such as a printer, mouse and external modem. Most new computers have two USB ports.

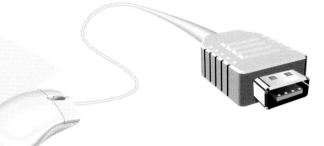

NETWORK PORT

A network port is found on a network interface card and allows you to connect the computer to a network. The two most popular types of network ports are the coax and RJ-45 ports. A coax port is a small, metal connector. An RJ-45 port looks like a large telephone jack.

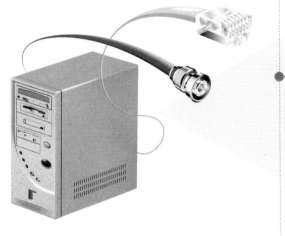

SCSI PORT

A Small Computer System Interface (SCSI, pronounced "scuzzy") port is a female connector with 50 or 68 holes. A SCSI port allows you to use a SCSI cable with a 50 or 68-pin male connector to connect devices such as an external hard drive, tape drive or scanner to the computer.

INTERNAL CONNECTORS

Most internal connectors in new computers are located on the system board, but some are found on expansion cards.

Most internal devices connect to the computer using a ribbon cable. The connector on the ribbon cable must be properly aligned with the connector on the system board or expansion card.

Many internal connectors have a pin missing to help you properly align the two connectors. Many connectors also have a plastic enclosure, which helps ensure the connectors are joined properly.

Ribbon Cable

Internal Connector

EIDE

An Enhanced Integrated Drive Electronics (EIDE) connector is a 40-pin male connector. Many new computers have two EIDE connectors. An EIDE connector allows you to use an EIDE ribbon cable to connect two devices, such as a hard drive and CD-ROM drive, to the computer.

SCSI

An internal Small Computer System Interface (SCSI) connector is a 50-pin male connector and is usually found on a SCSI expansion card. An internal SCSI connector allows you to use a SCSI ribbon cable to connect multiple storage devices, such as a hard drive and tape drive, to the computer.

FLOPPY DRIVE

A floppy drive connector is a 34-pin male connector. All computers have a floppy drive connector. A floppy drive connector allows you to use a floppy drive ribbon cable to connect two devices, such as a floppy drive and a tape drive, to the computer.

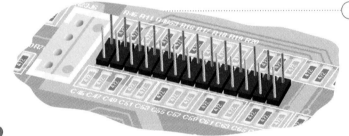

PARALLEL

An internal parallel connector is a 26-pin male connector. You can use an internal parallel connector to connect a parallel port to the computer. Many new computers do not have an internal parallel connector because the parallel port is built into the system board.

SERIAL

An internal serial connector is a 10-pin male connector. You can use an internal serial connector to connect a serial port to the computer. Many new computers do not have an internal serial connector because the serial port is built into the system board.

REFERENCE MATERIAL

WHERE CAN I FIND INFORMATION ABOUT MY COMPUTER AND THE TYPE OF UPGRADE OR REPAIR I WANT TO PERFORM?

There are many sources of reference material about upgrading and repairing computers.

SOURCES OF REFERENCE MATERIAL

DOCUMENTATION

When gathering reference material, you should start by reviewing the documentation that came with the computer. Computer documentation usually contains information about common error messages and often has a troubleshooting section that can help you solve common problems. This type of reference material is often provided in a printed manual, but may also be found on floppy disks or a CD-ROM disc.

INTERNET

The Internet is an excellent source of up-to-date reference material about computers. Almost all computer manufacturers have Web sites where you can review product information and contact technical support representatives. Many individuals also have Web pages you can visit to find information about upgrading and repairing computers.

Computer-related newsgroups are another good source of reference material on the Internet.

COMPUTER CLUBS

Joining a computer club in your area allows you to exchange ideas with other people who are interested in computer upgrade and repair. Some computer clubs offer classes on computer maintenance and repair.

COMPUTER SHOWS

Computer shows, where manufacturers display and sell computer hardware and software, are a good source of information. At these shows, you can speak with people who are knowledgeable about upgrading and repairing computers. Many computer shows also provide workshops that teach you how to perform basic computer maintenance and repair.

CD-ROM DISCS

CD-ROM discs are available that contain computer reference material. For example, you can purchase a CD-ROM disc that contains frequently asked questions about computer repair or a collection of magazine articles related to computer hardware and software. You can also find product specifications, hardware settings and solutions to common computer problems on CD-ROM discs.

PREPARE TO UPGRADE OR REPAIR A COMPUTER

WHAT CAN I DO TO PREPARE TO UPGRADE OR REPAIR MY COMPUTER?

There are several things you can do to prepare for an upgrade or repair. Proper preparation can help make upgrading or repairing your computer easier.

SCHEDULE TIME

You should schedule an upgrade or repair for a time when you will not need your computer. You may want to choose a time when sources of help and technical support are available.

When scheduling an upgrade or repair, make sure you set aside enough time to complete the task. Replacing or adding a component may not take very long, but setting up the computer to work with a new component can be time-consuming. You should also allow time for any problems that may arise.

RECORD THE COMPUTER SETTINGS

The computer settings store information about the devices installed on a computer and are essential to the proper functioning of the computer. You should write down the computer settings before you begin to upgrade or repair a computer, as this information may be erased during the upgrade or repair. For information on computer settings, see page 168.

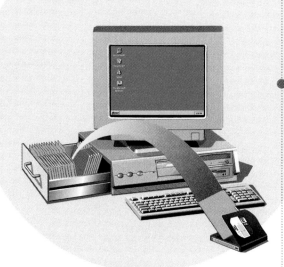

BACK UP INFORMATION

When you upgrade or repair a computer, you risk losing or damaging information stored on the computer. No matter what type of upgrade or repair you are performing, you should make a backup copy of the information stored on the computer. For more information, see page 158.

GATHER SOFTWARE

Before beginning an upgrade or repair, you should make sure you have a startup disk, the installation disks or CD-ROM disc for the operating system and the installation disks for the backup software. In the event of a problem, such as a hard drive failure, you may need to re-install the operating system and backup software before you can restore your information.

GATHER REFERENCE MATERIAL

You should gather any reference material you will need to perform the upgrade or repair, such as the documentation that came with the computer or component. You may need to refer to this information if a problem arises.

GATHER EQUIPMENT

Before you begin upgrading or repairing a computer, you should make sure you have all the necessary equipment to perform the task, such as cables or software. You should also gather any computer tools you may need. For information on computer tools, see page 6.

PROTECT COMPONENTS FROM STATIC ELECTRICITY

Static electricity can damage the components in a computer. When upgrading or repairing a computer, you should take precautions to protect the components from damage caused by static electricity. For more information, see page 8.

PREPARE A WORK AREA

Clear a work area where you can perform the upgrade or repair. Disassembling a computer can be awkward and usually requires a lot of space. If your computer is in a cramped location, you should move it to a more accessible area. You should choose a well-lit area so you can clearly see the inside of the computer.

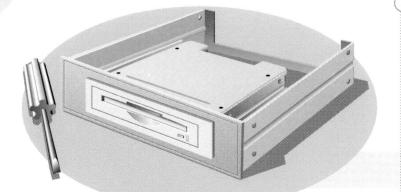

PREPARE COMPONENTS

Many components require some assembly before they can be installed in a computer. For example, you may need to attach a mounting bracket to a storage device before you can install it. Consult the documentation included with the component to determine if assembly is required.

TAKE NOTES AND MAKE DRAWINGS

While disassembling a computer, you should take notes and make drawings. For example, you should record information such as where cables are connected, the order you remove components and how jumpers and switches are set on components. This information can help you later reassemble the computer.

RECORD MODEL AND SERIAL NUMBERS

You should record the model and serial numbers of all the components in your computer. An accurate listing of this information can help make upgrading and repairing the computer an easier task.

TRAINING FOR COMPUTER UPGRADE AND REPAIR

HOW CAN TRAINING HELP ME UPGRADE AND REPAIR MY COMPUTER?

Training will teach you how to upgrade and repair your computer more efficiently.

One of the best ways to learn about upgrading and repairing a computer is to work on your own computer to gain hands-on experience.

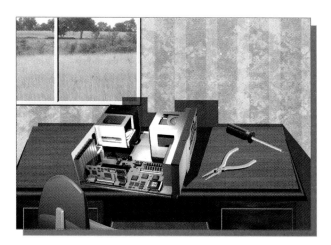

BENEFITS OF TRAINING

Learning how to upgrade and repair a computer allows you to effectively troubleshoot computer problems you experience and enables you to customize your computer to suit your needs. The ability to upgrade and repair your computer also saves you from having to find a reliable repair service and can save you money.

Keep up-to-date on the latest trends!

USA $3.25
Canada $5.95

Hardware reviews and much more!

UP-TO-DATE INFORMATION

You should continue to educate yourself on new developments in the computer industry after you finish your training. The information you learn while training can become obsolete if you do not keep up-to-date with current computer products, trends and information. Computer magazines, which are available at most computer stores, are good sources of current information.

TYPES OF TRAINING

COMPUTER STORES

Many computer stores, especially large chain stores, offer classes in computer upgrade and repair. The classes are usually inexpensive and some stores even offer free classes to regular customers.

COMPUTER AND BUSINESS SCHOOLS

Many specialized schools, such as computer and business schools, offer computer upgrade and repair classes. You may be able to receive certification when you complete a training course at a computer or business school.

COMPUTER-BASED TRAINING

Computer-Based Training (CBT) allows you to use your computer to learn at home at your own pace. Computer-based training courses are available in a package containing a book and CD-ROM disc at most computer stores. You can also find courses on the Internet.

Computer-based training courses contain step-by-step instructions with detailed illustrations and diagrams. There are also questions you can answer to receive feedback about your progress. You may be able to receive certification when you complete computer-based training.

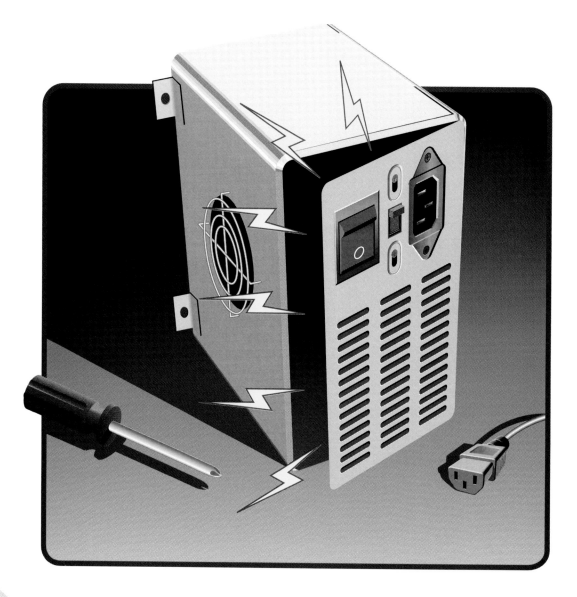

CHAPTER 2

COMPUTER ESSENTIALS

Before you start an upgrade or repair, familiarize yourself with the components a computer requires to operate. This chapter explains the system board, central processing unit and much more.

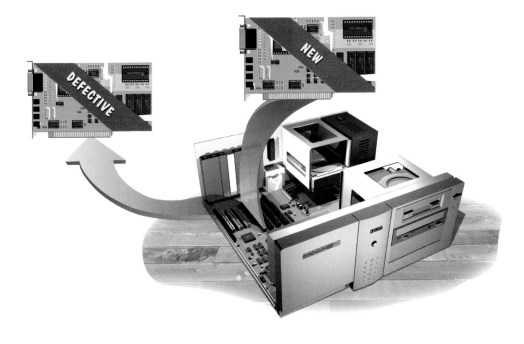

A computer case is a box that contains most of the major components of a computer system. A computer case provides a solid structure that protects components from dirt and damage.

When upgrading or repairing a computer, you will often need to remove the computer case cover.

REMOVE A COMPUTER CASE COVER

Before removing the computer case cover, turn off the computer and unplug the power cable.

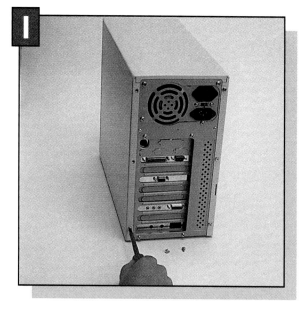

Remove the screws that hold the computer case cover in place. Most covers are held in place by 4 screws at the back of the computer.

You can check your computer's documentation to determine which screws to remove. Some of the screws at the back of the computer secure internal devices, such as the power supply, to the computer.

Slide the cover backward or forward a short distance. Then lift the cover straight up.

CONSIDERATIONS

COMPUTER CASE STYLE

WHAT SHOULD I CONSIDER WHEN CHOOSING A COMPUTER CASE?

There are two main styles of computer cases—desktop and tower. A desktop case is wider than it is tall and usually sits on a desk, under a monitor.

Desktop Case

A tower case often sits on the floor. This provides more desk space, but can be less convenient for inserting and removing floppy disks and CD-ROM discs.

Tower Case

FORM FACTOR

A form factor is a set of specifications that determines the internal size and shape of a computer case. The two most popular computer case form factors are ATX and Baby AT. The computer case must use the same form factor as the power supply and system board.

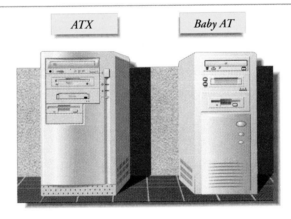

ATX   *Baby AT*

SET UP

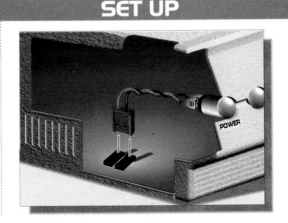

Do I need to set up my new computer case?

Most computer cases have items, such as a keylock and power button, which attach to connectors on the system board. Although the connectors look very similar, your computer will have problems if you attach an item to the wrong connectors. Make sure you check all the connections carefully.

SYSTEM BOARD

A system board is the largest and most complex component in a computer.

Before replacing a system board, turn off the computer, unplug the power cable and remove the cover from the computer case. Then ground yourself and the computer case. For information on grounding, see page 8.

1

Disconnect the cables from the back of the computer. Then remove the expansion cards from the system board.

2

Disconnect all the cables from the system board.

3

Remove all the screws that secure the system board in the computer case.

4

Slide the system board slightly sideways to release the small plastic spacers, called standoffs, that prevent the system board from touching the computer case. Then lift the system board out of the computer case.

5

If necessary, add the standoffs from the old system board to the new system board.

6

Place the new system board in the computer case, slide the system board into position and secure it with screws. Then reconnect all the cables, reinstall the expansion cards and replace the cover on the computer case.

SYSTEM BOARD COMPONENTS

What are the main components on a system board?

● A **port** allows the system board to communicate with an external device, such as a printer.

● A memory slot is a socket on the system board. A memory module, which holds memory chips for storing data, sits in a memory slot.

● A chipset is a series of chips that contains instructions for controlling the movement of data through the system board.

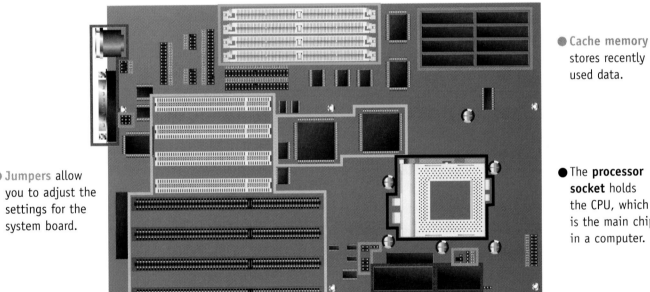

● Cache memory stores recently used data.

● Jumpers allow you to adjust the settings for the system board.

● The **processor socket** holds the CPU, which is the main chip in a computer.

● An expansion slot is a socket on the system board. An expansion card, which lets you add features to a computer, plugs into an expansion slot.

● The **Basic Input/Output System (BIOS) chip** controls the transfer of data between devices attached to the system board.

● The **Complementary Metal Oxide Semiconductor (CMOS) chip** saves the time and the computer's BIOS settings. A battery provides power to the CMOS chip when the computer is turned off.

SYSTEM BOARD

CONSIDERATIONS

WHAT SHOULD I CONSIDER WHEN CHOOSING A SYSTEM BOARD?

FORM FACTOR

A form factor is a set of specifications that determines the general size and shape of a system board. The two main types of form factors are Baby AT and ATX. The system board must use the same form factor as the computer case and power supply.

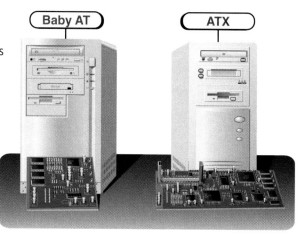

Baby AT

ATX

PROCESSOR SOCKET

The type of processor socket on the system board determines the type of CPU you can use in the computer. A square, two-inch socket, called Socket 7, holds a Pentium CPU. The Pentium II CPU fits into a socket similar to an expansion slot, called Slot 1.

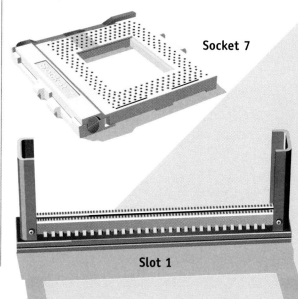

Socket 7

Slot 1

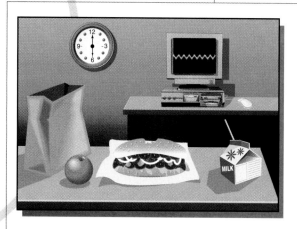

POWER MANAGEMENT

Most system boards offer Advanced Power Management (APM) features. These features allow you to conserve energy by controlling how a computer uses power after a period of inactivity. For example, APM allows you to have your hard drive, monitor and other devices shut down when they are not in use.

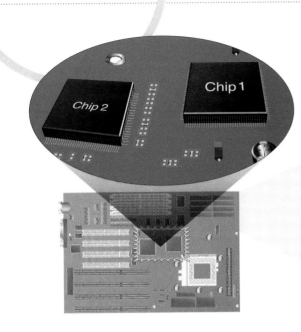

CHIPSET

Each system board has a series of chips that contains instructions to control the movement of data through the system board. When you purchase a system board, make sure the chipset on the system board is compatible with your CPU, otherwise the computer will not work properly.

CACHE MEMORY

Cache memory is used to speed up the transfer of data by storing data the computer has recently used. Cache memory is faster and more expensive than main memory. Most new system boards come with 512 K of cache memory.

MEMORY SPEED

The speed at which information is stored and accessed in memory is called access time and is measured in nanoseconds (ns). Many system boards can only use memory that has an access time of 60 or 70 ns.

When upgrading your system board, make sure the system board supports the access time of your existing memory, otherwise you will also have to upgrade the memory.

SYSTEM BOARD

BUS

INTERNAL BUS

WHAT ARE THE MOST COMMON BUS TYPES ON A SYSTEM BOARD?

The internal bus carries data between components on the system board, such as memory and the CPU. The speed at which a bus can carry data is measured in megahertz (MHz). Most system boards have an internal bus speed of 66 MHz. Many new system boards can use bus speeds of 83 and 100 MHz.

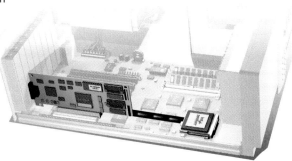

EXPANSION BUS

An expansion bus carries data between devices in a computer.

ISA

The Industry Standard Architecture (ISA) bus is the slowest and oldest type of expansion bus. This bus is often used to transfer data to and from a slow device, such as a modem.

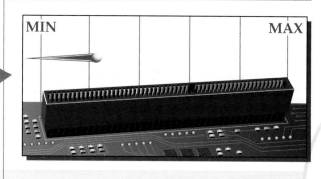

AGP

The Accelerated Graphics Port (AGP) expansion bus is designed to carry complex data between an AGP video card and the computer's memory.

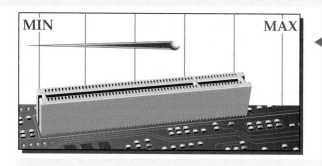

PCI

The Peripheral Component Interconnect (PCI) bus is the most commonly used type of expansion bus. The PCI bus is used to communicate with a high-speed device, such as a hard drive.

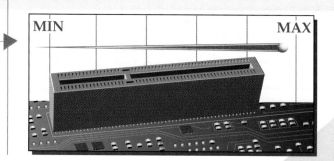

BIOS

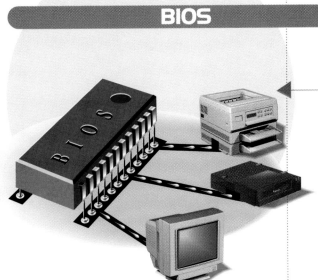

What does the BIOS chip do?

The Basic Input/Output System (BIOS) chip controls the transfer of data between devices attached to the system board. When you turn on the computer, the BIOS chip automatically examines each device and adjusts the system board settings to ensure the devices work properly. This allows the computer to set itself up automatically each time a new device is added or an existing device is removed.

How do I access and change the BIOS settings for my computer?

To access the BIOS settings, you can use configuration software or press a specific key combination as your computer starts. For more information on BIOS settings, see page 168.

Can I upgrade the BIOS chip on my system board?

Manufacturers frequently update BIOS chips to correct problems or enhance the performance of the chips. You may be able to upgrade an older BIOS chip to a new version using a software program.

TROUBLESHOOT AND MAINTAIN

Is there software I can use to test my system board?

Diagnostic software allows you to test your system board. For example, diagnostic software can help you determine if all the ports on the computer are working properly. You can purchase diagnostic software at most computer stores.

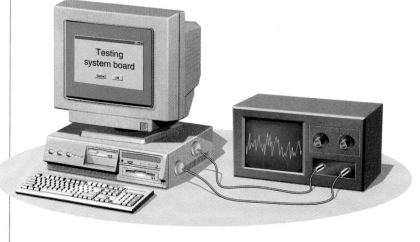

How can I determine if my system board's settings are correct?

Check the documentation included with your system board or computer to determine if the system board settings are correct. Incorrect system board settings, such as an incorrect bus speed, can cause problems with the computer, such as a lockup or failure to start.

My system board is not working properly. What should I do?

A problem with a system board is usually caused by a malfunctioning component, such as a faulty memory module. To find the component causing the problem, remove a component not required for basic operation and then start the computer to determine if the problem still exists. Repeat this procedure until you discover which component is causing the problem.

My system board is not faulty. Why am I experiencing problems?

Although problems such as computer lockups and memory errors resemble problems caused by a faulty system board, they may actually be caused by a loss of power. To protect a computer from a loss of power, you can purchase an Uninterruptible Power Supply (UPS).

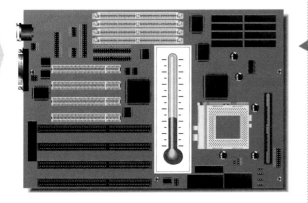

How do I prevent my computer from overheating?

The CPU and other components inside the computer case generate heat. Overheating may cause the computer to malfunction. To prevent overheating, make sure the fan inside the computer is working properly. Many new system boards have a built-in thermometer that will shut down the computer before it overheats.

How do I clean my system board?

You can use a can of compressed air to blow away the dust and dirt on your system board. If the system board is extremely dusty, you may need to remove the cables and components from the system board before cleaning.

POWER SUPPLY

A power supply changes the alternating current (AC) that comes from an electrical outlet to the direct current (DC) that a computer can use.

Before replacing a power supply, turn off the computer, unplug the power cable and remove the cover from the computer case. Then ground yourself and the computer case. For information on grounding, see page 8.

Disconnect the power supply cables from the system board and other devices inside the computer.

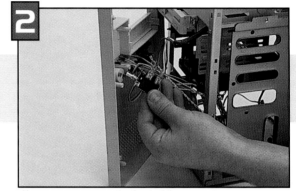

If necessary, remove the front of the computer case and unfasten the power switch from the front of the computer.

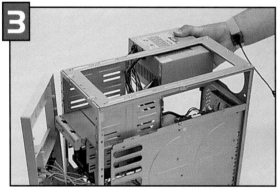

Remove the screws that secure the power supply in the computer case. Then slide the power supply out of the computer case.

Slide the new power supply into the computer case and use screws to secure it.

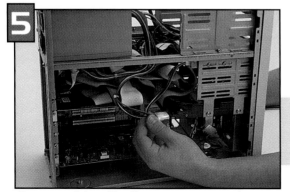

Reconnect all the cables. If necessary, reconnect the power switch and replace the front of the computer case. Then replace the cover on the computer case.

REPLACEMENT CONSIDERATIONS

How do I know when I need to replace my power supply?

Power supplies tend to be very reliable and usually work for many years without any problems. Symptoms of a faulty power supply can include the computer locking up repeatedly or other components failing to work consistently.

Before replacing a power supply, make sure the problems you are experiencing are not caused by another component. Some problems you think are due to a faulty power supply may actually be caused by another component, such as a malfunctioning hard drive.

What safety precautions should I take when replacing a power supply?

In addition to unplugging the power supply from the electrical outlet on your wall, you should never take the cover off a power supply you are replacing. Even when the power supply is not plugged into an electrical outlet, it can still contain power.

CONSIDERATIONS

WHAT SHOULD I CONSIDER WHEN CHOOSING A POWER SUPPLY?

WATTAGE

The capacity of a power supply is measured in watts. A power supply with a capacity of 250 watts is more than enough for a typical computer.

ENERGY EFFICIENCY

Some new power supplies are capable of turning themselves off after a period of inactivity to conserve energy. When the computer is needed again, this type of power supply uses a small electrical charge to "wake up" the computer.

FORM FACTOR

A form factor is a set of specifications that determines the general size and shape of a power supply. There are two main types of form factors—Baby AT and ATX. The power supply must use the same form factor as the computer case and system board.

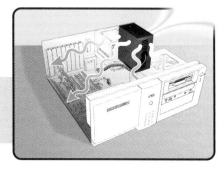

One important difference between form factors is the fan. The fan in a Baby AT power supply pushes air out of the computer. The fan in an ATX power supply draws air into the computer, which cools the power supply and other computer components more efficiently.

VOLTAGE SELECTOR

The electrical system in North America provides power at 110 volts. Other areas of the world have electrical systems that provide power at 220 volts. Many power supplies have a small switch that allows you to change between 110 and 220 volt electrical systems. Some new power supplies can sense the voltage and switch automatically.

MAINTAIN

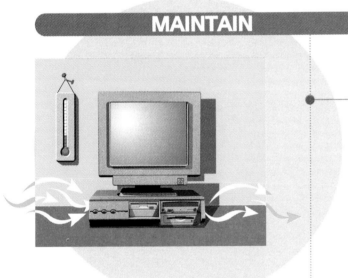

How can I prolong the life of my power supply?

The location of your computer can influence the way the power supply performs. You should keep your computer in a cool, dust-free environment to help prolong the life of the power supply and ensure the fan has cool, clean air to move through the computer case.

Do I need to clean my power supply?

Over time, dust can accumulate on the fan opening and on the back of the power supply. You can remove this dust with a computer vacuum cleaner. You should never cover the fan opening to prevent dust from gathering, as this can cause the power supply to overheat and your computer to shut down.

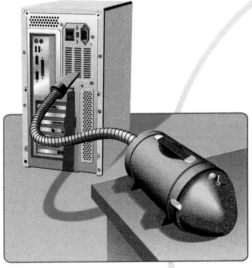

CPU

The Central Processing Unit (CPU) chip processes instructions, performs calculations and manages the flow of information through a computer system.

REPLACE A PENTIUM CPU

Before replacing a Pentium CPU, turn off the computer, unplug the power cable and remove the cover from the computer case. Then ground yourself and the computer case. For information on grounding, see page 8.

If necessary, disconnect the CPU fan's cable from the power supply.

If necessary, release the clip securing the CPU fan to the system board. Then lift the lever that secures the CPU in the socket.

Lift the CPU out of the socket.

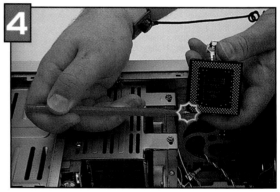

Align the beveled corner of the new CPU with the beveled corner on the socket. Then place the CPU in the socket.

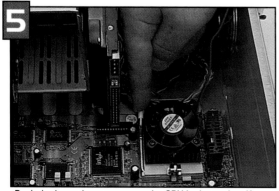

Push the lever down to secure the CPU in the socket. If necessary, use the clip to secure the CPU fan to the system board.

If necessary, connect the CPU fan's cable to the power supply. Then replace the cover on the computer case.

PENTIUM CONSIDERATIONS

WHAT SHOULD I CONSIDER WHEN CHOOSING A PENTIUM CPU?

MANUFACTURER

Intel's Pentium chip is the most popular CPU in its class. Comparable CPU chips include the 6x86 and MediaGX chips manufactured by Cyrix, as well as the AMD-K5 chip manufactured by AMD.

SPEED

The speed of a CPU chip is measured in megahertz (MHz), or millions of cycles per second. The faster the speed of the CPU chip, the faster the computer can operate. Common speeds for Intel's Pentium chips include 90, 133, 166 and 200 MHz. Many Pentium chips with speeds of 166 MHz and higher support MMX technology, which provides improved multimedia performance.

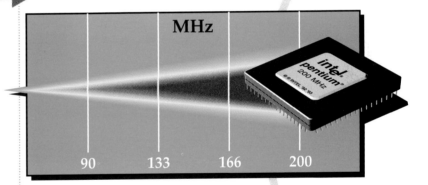

SOCKET TYPE

You can only install a Pentium or comparable CPU chip on a system board that has a square, two-inch socket, called Socket 7.

REPLACE A PENTIUM II CPU

Before replacing a Pentium II CPU, turn off the computer, unplug the power cable and remove the cover from the computer case. Then ground yourself and the computer case. For information on grounding, see page 8.

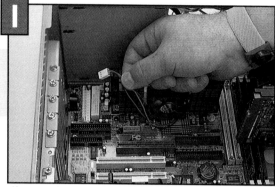

If necessary, disconnect the CPU fan's cable from the system board.

Push the clips on each end of the CPU inward and then lift the CPU out of the slot.

Place the new CPU in the guide rails for the slot and then press down firmly and evenly across the top of the CPU until it is securely inserted in the slot.

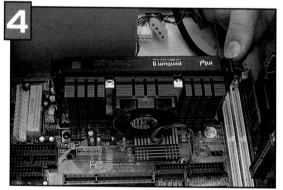

Push the clips on each end of the CPU outward until the clips snap into place.

If necessary, connect the CPU fan's cable to the system board. Then replace the cover on the computer case.

PENTIUM II CONSIDERATIONS

WHAT SHOULD I CONSIDER WHEN CHOOSING A PENTIUM II CPU?

MANUFACTURER

Intel's Pentium II chip is the most popular CPU chip in its class. Comparable CPU chips include the 6x86MX and M II chips made by Cyrix and the AMD-K6 chip made by AMD.

SPEED

The speed of a CPU chip is measured in megahertz (MHz), or millions of cycles per second. The faster the speed of the CPU chip, the faster the computer can operate. Intel's Pentium II chips are available with speeds of 233, 266, 300, 333, 350 and 400 MHz. All Pentium II chips support MMX technology, which provides improved multimedia performance.

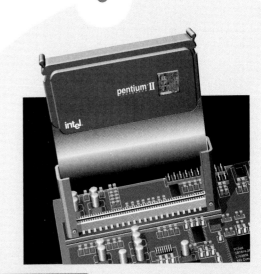

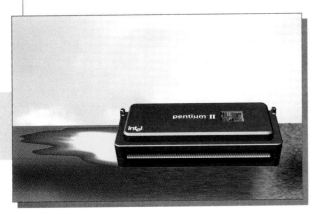

SLOT TYPE

You can only install Intel's Pentium II chip on a system board that has a slot similar in appearance to an expansion slot, called Slot 1.

Comparable CPU chips may require a square, two-inch socket, called Socket 7.

OTHER TYPES OF CPUs

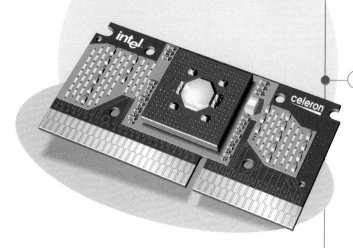

CELERON

The Celeron chip is a fast and inexpensive CPU chip made by Intel. Celeron chips are similar to Pentium II chips, but have less built-in memory. The Celeron chip is designed to meet the needs and budgets of most new home computer users.

Celeron chips are available with speeds of 266, 300 and 333 MHz.

PENTIUM PRO

Intel's Pentium Pro chip is ideal for computers that use powerful operating systems, such as Windows NT and UNIX. Pentium Pro chips are available with speeds of 150, 166, 180 and 200 MHz.

The successor to the Pentium Pro chip is called the Pentium II Xeon.

FUTURE CPUs

Intel's next generation of CPUs is expected to go well beyond the speed of the current Pentium II chips. This new CPU generation, currently named Merced, is being designed primarily for use in powerful network computers.

TROUBLESHOOT

After installing my new CPU, do I need to adjust any settings on the system board?

You may need to adjust jumpers or switches on the system board to indicate the speed of your new CPU. If there are no jumpers or switches for the fastest speed of your CPU, your system board may not support that speed. To take advantage of the speed your new CPU offers, you may need to upgrade the system board.

I have installed a new CPU and now my computer freezes shortly after I turn it on. What is wrong?

The new CPU may be overheating. To determine if an overheating CPU is the cause of the problem, adjust the jumpers or switches on the system board to reduce the speed of the CPU. If your computer operates properly at the reduced CPU speed, the CPU fan may not have been able to sufficiently cool the CPU. You should replace the CPU fan with a larger fan.

MEMORY

Memory temporarily stores data in a computer. The main memory in a computer is called Random Access Memory (RAM).

A **memory module** is a small circuit board that holds memory chips. A memory module connects to a socket on a system board using small metal pads, called pins.

A **memory chip** stores data used by the computer.

A **memory bank** is a section of sockets on a system board.

MEMORY MODULES

WHAT TYPES OF MEMORY MODULES ARE AVAILABLE?

SIMM

A Single In-line Memory Module (SIMM) is the most common type of memory module. SIMMs can have either 30 or 72 pins, but the 72-pin module is more common in new computers.

A bank of SIMMs usually consists of two sockets, so you must install two SIMMs at a time.

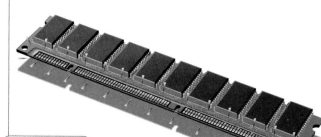

30 pin

72 pin

DIMM

A Dual In-line Memory Module (DIMM) is used in computers with a Pentium or compatible CPU. A DIMM is similar to a SIMM, but has 168 pins.

A bank of DIMMs consists of only one socket, so you only need to install one DIMM at a time.

TYPES OF MEMORY

WHAT TYPES OF MEMORY ARE AVAILABLE?

DRAM

Dynamic RAM (DRAM) is inexpensive and is the most popular type of main memory used in computers.

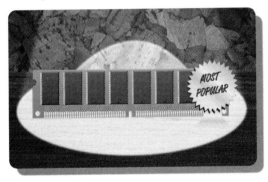

MOST POPULAR

EDO DRAM

Extended Data Out DRAM (EDO DRAM) is slightly faster than FPM DRAM.

SRAM

Static RAM (SRAM) is efficient and fast, but is very expensive. SRAM is used in small amounts as cache memory in a computer. Cache memory improves the performance of a computer by storing data the computer frequently uses.

RECENTLY USED DATA

FPM DRAM

Fast Page Mode DRAM (FPM DRAM) is a slow type of DRAM that is not often used in today's computers.

FPM DRAM

SDRAM

Synchronous DRAM (SDRAM) is a very fast type of main memory often used in new computers.

INSTALL SIMMs

Before installing SIMMs, turn off the computer, unplug the power cable and remove the cover from the computer case. Then ground yourself and the computer case. For information on grounding, see page 8.

1 Disconnect any cables inside the computer that restrict access to the memory sockets.

2 Locate the empty socket closest to the back of the bank where you want to install the SIMM. Then locate the key on the side of the socket and the notch on the side of the memory module. To ensure you install the memory module correctly, align the key with the notch.

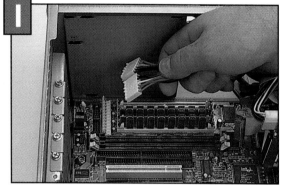

3 Place the SIMM in the socket at a 45-degree angle.

4 Gently move the SIMM into an upright position until the clips on each end of the socket snap into place to secure the SIMM in the socket.

5 Repeat steps 2 to 4 to install the second SIMM.

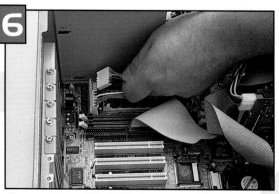

6 Reconnect any cables inside the computer. Then replace the cover on the computer case.

INSTALL A DIMM

Before installing a DIMM, turn off the computer, unplug the power cable and remove the cover from the computer case. Then ground yourself and the computer case. For information on grounding, see page 8.

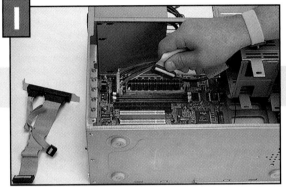

Disconnect any cables inside the computer that restrict access to the memory sockets.

Push the clips on each end of the socket out of the way.

Locate the key on the side of the socket and the notch on the side of the memory module. To ensure you install the memory module correctly, align the key with the notch.

Push down firmly and evenly across the top of the memory module to insert it in the socket.

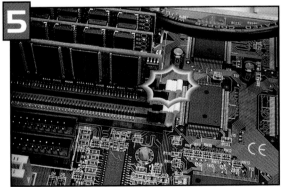

The clips snap into place to secure the DIMM in the socket.

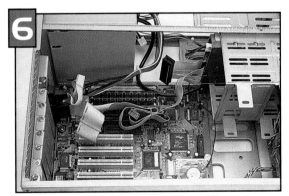

Reconnect any cables inside the computer. Then replace the cover on the computer case.

CONSIDERATIONS

WHAT SHOULD I CONSIDER WHEN CHOOSING MEMORY?

IDENTIFICATION

Most memory modules look very similar. This makes it difficult to identify the type of memory used in a computer. To determine the type of memory your computer uses, refer to the documentation included with your computer or system board.

IBM

INTEL

KINGSTON

ACCESS TIME

The speed at which information is stored and accessed in memory is called access time and is measured in nanoseconds (ns). The lower the access time, the faster the memory.

Most system boards using SIMMs support memory with an access time of 70 ns or faster.

PENTIUM II

4 GB Hard Drive

Ergonomic Keyboard

CONTENTS FRAGILE

32 MB MEMORY

Access Time

70 ns

MEMORY SIZE

Memory is measured in megabytes (MB). Computers are commonly sold with 16 or 32 MB of memory. You can improve the performance of a computer by adding more memory. Although most computers can hold at least 128 MB of memory, the capabilities of the system board may limit the amount of memory you can add.

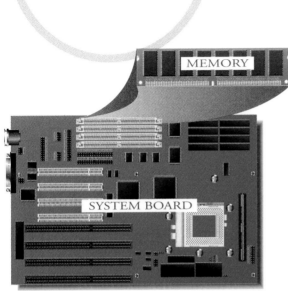

SYSTEM BOARD COMPATIBILITY

When purchasing memory, you must ensure the memory is compatible with the system board. The system board determines the type of memory modules required, as well as the access time of the memory. If you install a memory module that has an incompatible access time, the system board will not work properly.

PARITY CHECKING

Parity checking is a system used to ensure information is stored properly in the computer's memory. Invalid data in the memory can result in errors such as a system failure.

New computers are much more reliable than older computers, so newer computers no longer support parity checking. Before purchasing memory, you should determine whether your computer uses parity or non-parity SIMMs.

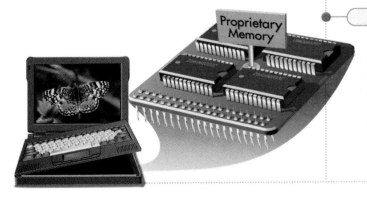

PROPRIETARY

Proprietary memory is designed for use with a specific type of computer. For example, you cannot use proprietary memory designed for a notebook computer in a desktop computer. Many notebook computers and high-end computers, such as servers, use proprietary memory.

TROUBLESHOOT

Can I install memory modules made by different manufacturers?

Installing memory modules made by different manufacturers can cause problems such as memory read and write errors. You should always install memory modules made by the same manufacturer.

What happens if I break a clip when installing a memory module?

When installing a memory module, be careful not to break the clips that secure the memory module in place. If you break a clip, it may be impossible to install the memory module correctly, which could make the system board unusable.

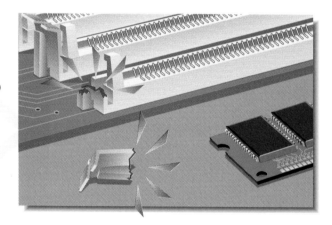

Should I test the new memory I installed?

After installing memory, you should perform a burn in for up to 48 hours. A burn in involves testing the memory for a long period of time to ensure it works properly. For example, you could set up your computer to repeatedly perform a memory-intensive task, such as a complicated spreadsheet calculation.

I just installed new memory. Why did I get a memory error message?

Memory chips are very susceptible to damage from static electricity. If you handled a memory module without properly grounding yourself, static electricity may have damaged the memory chips on the module. For information on protecting components from static electricity, see page 8.

How do I troubleshoot a memory error?

Memory errors are often difficult to troubleshoot because they are similar to problems caused by other components. If you suspect the problems you are experiencing are due to memory errors, you may be able to correct the problem by removing and then re-inserting a memory module in a socket.

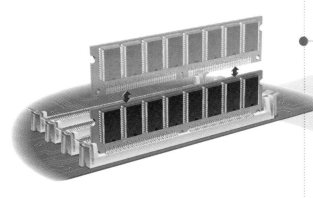

Is there a device I can use to verify that a memory module is working properly?

There is a device you can use to verify if a memory module is working properly. Although this device is very expensive to buy, some computer stores may have the device and will test a memory module for you.

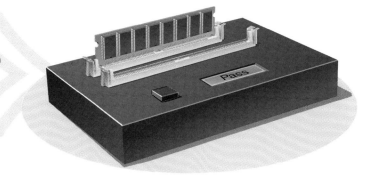

EXPANSION CARD

An expansion card is a circuit board in a computer that provides improved or additional features.

Before replacing an expansion card, turn off the computer, unplug the power cable and remove the computer case cover. Then ground yourself and the computer case. For information on grounding, see page 8.

1

Disconnect any cables attached to the expansion card at the back of the computer and remove the screw securing the card to the computer case.

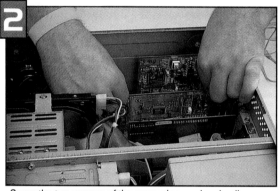

2

Grasp the top corners of the expansion card and pull straight up to remove the card from the slot.

3

Remove any cables connecting the card to other components inside the computer.

4

Use cables to attach other components to the new expansion card.

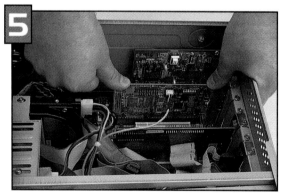

5

Place the expansion card in the slot. Press down firmly and evenly across the top of the card until it is securely inserted in the expansion slot.

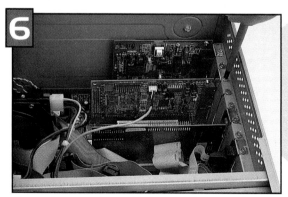

6

Secure the expansion card to the computer case using a small screw. Then replace the cover on the computer case.

SET UP

List of Resources

	IRQ	DMA
Printer Port	7	0
Serial Port	4	-
Sound Card	5	1

Do I have to change any settings for my new expansion card?

Expansion cards require several computer resources, such as Interrupt Request (IRQ) settings. Before installing an expansion card, make sure you have a list of the resources used by other devices. If the expansion card requires the same resources as another device, you may need to change the settings for the card. Most expansion cards come with an installation program you can use to change the settings. For information on resource settings, see page 164.

What are Plug and Play expansion cards?

New computers and expansion cards use Plug and Play technology. When you install a Plug and Play expansion card, the computer may automatically detect and set up the card for you.

UPGRADE

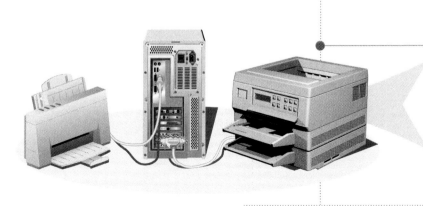

Can I use expansion cards to upgrade my computer?

If your computer does not have enough ports for all the devices you want to connect, you can install an expansion card to add an extra port. For example, you can install an expansion card to add an extra parallel port to the computer.

EXPANSION CARD

CONSIDERATIONS

WHAT SHOULD I CONSIDER WHEN CHOOSING AN EXPANSION CARD?

EXPANSION SLOT TYPE

The type of expansion card you can use depends on the type of expansion slots in your computer. An expansion slot is a socket on the system board where you insert an expansion card. The most common types of expansion slots are Industry Standard Architecture (ISA) and Peripheral Component Interconnect (PCI). Most new computers contain both types of expansion slots.

LENGTH

Expansion cards vary in length. Complex expansion cards that contain many chips and components may take up the entire length of the computer. These long expansion cards are called full-length cards. Smaller cards, referred to as half-length cards, are more common.

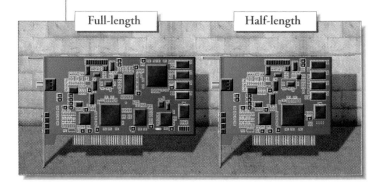

Full-length   Half-length

COST

The cost of expansion cards varies, depending on the type and quality of the card. Although some expansion cards are expensive, adding or upgrading an expansion card can be one of the most economical ways to keep your computer up-to-date.

TROUBLESHOOT AND MAINTAIN

How can I test an expansion card?

Many expansion cards include testing software you can use to ensure the card is installed correctly. If an expansion card does not include testing software, you should use a simple procedure to test the device. For example, if you are installing a new parallel port, you can test the port by printing a text file.

I think my expansion card is malfunctioning. How can I confirm this?

If an expansion card is not working, you can ensure the card is the cause of the problem by removing the card and replacing it with a card you know works properly.

How do I clean my expansion cards?

Expansion cards can become dusty and may require occasional cleaning. Remove the computer case cover and carefully use a computer vacuum cleaner or can of compressed air to remove dust from the card. For more information on cleaning a computer, see page 154.

CHAPTER 3

INPUT AND OUTPUT DEVICES

Input devices allow you to communicate with your computer, while output devices allow your computer to communicate with you. Learn about keyboards, sound cards, digital cameras and more in this chapter.

POINTING DEVICE

A pointing device allows you to select and move items on the screen. The mouse is the most common type of pointing device.

CONNECT A POINTING DEVICE

Before connecting a pointing device, turn off the computer.

Position the pointing device where you can use it comfortably.

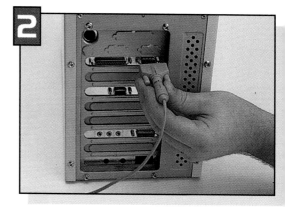

Connect the cable from the pointing device to a serial port at the back of the computer. On new computers, the mouse may connect to a mouse port.

UPGRADE AND MAINTAIN A MOUSE

What kind of mouse can I upgrade to?

You can purchase a new mouse with improved capabilities, such as buttons you can program to perform a specific action or a wheel between the left and right buttons that lets you quickly scroll through information.

How do I know when to clean my mouse?

The ball inside a mouse collects dirt and debris from a desk or mouse pad. If your mouse pointer is hard to position and sticks on the screen, you may need to clean the mouse. Follow the manufacturer's instructions for cleaning the mouse.

OTHER TYPES OF POINTING DEVICES

A mouse does not suit my needs. What other types of pointing devices are available?

TRACKBALL

A trackball is an upside-down mouse that remains stationary on your desk. You can roll the ball with your thumb, fingers or palm to move the mouse pointer on the screen. A trackball is useful when you have limited desk space.

TOUCHPAD

A touchpad is a surface that is sensitive to pressure and motion. You can tap the surface of the touchpad with your finger or press a button to perform an action such as a click.

POINTING STICK

A pointing stick resembles the eraser on the end of a pencil. The mouse pointer moves in the direction you push the pointing stick. Pointing sticks also have buttons, similar to mouse buttons, you can press to perform an action such as a click.

KEYBOARD

A keyboard allows you to enter information and instructions into a computer.

CONNECT A KEYBOARD

Before connecting a keyboard, turn off the computer.

Position the keyboard where you can use it comfortably.

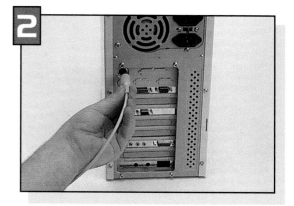

Connect the cable from the keyboard to the keyboard port at the back of the computer.

SET UP

5 - Pin

6 - Pin

The cable connector does not fit the keyboard port on my computer. What should I do?

The cable connector may be a 5-pin DIN connector. Many newer computers require a smaller 6-pin mini-DIN connector, also called a PS/2 connector. You can buy an adapter which will allow you to use either type of connector.

Do I need to install a driver for my keyboard?

All operating systems can automatically detect and set up a keyboard you connect. The operating system can also install the necessary driver for you. A driver is the software that allows the computer's operating system to communicate with and control the keyboard.

Keyboards that have built-in enhancements, such as trackballs, may require you to install additional drivers. The additional drivers are included with the keyboard.

UPGRADE

WHAT KIND OF KEYBOARD CAN I UPGRADE TO?

WIRELESS

Wireless keyboards do not use a cable to connect to a computer. A wireless keyboard uses an infrared transmitter and receiver to communicate with a computer.

ERGONOMIC

Ergonomically designed keyboards position your hands naturally and support your wrists so you can work more comfortably.

BUILT-IN ENHANCEMENTS

Many new keyboards include built-in enhancements such as trackballs, microphones, speakers and volume controls.

MAINTAIN

HOW DO I CLEAN MY KEYBOARD?

Over time, dust and dirt can accumulate on a keyboard, causing the keys to stick or not respond when pressed. To remove dust and dirt, you can run a computer vacuum cleaner over the keys. If vacuuming does not work, you can use a can of compressed air to blow out any dirt embedded in your keyboard.

The plastic outer surface of the keyboard can be cleaned with a damp cloth. You should not attempt to open your keyboard to clean the inside, as this can damage the keyboard.

63

A printer produces a paper copy of information generated by a computer.

Before connecting a printer, turn off the computer.

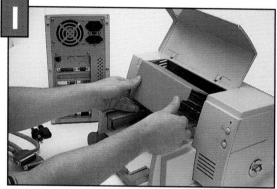

If necessary, remove any spacers or tape used to secure the printer's internal components during shipping. Then assemble the printer according to the instructions in the printer's documentation.

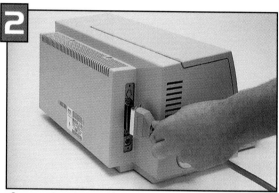

Connect the printer cable to the port at the back of the printer.

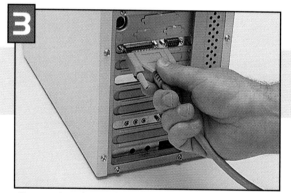

Connect the printer cable to a parallel port at the back of the computer.

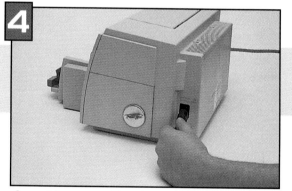

Connect the power cable to the power connector at the back of the printer.

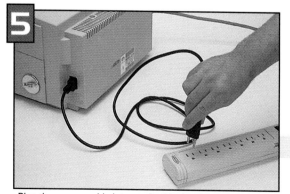

Plug the power cable into an electrical outlet.

SET UP

Which settings can I change for my printer?

You can change settings such as the paper size or ink cartridge the printer uses. Instead of using switches on the printer, some printers include a software program so you can use your computer to change the printer's settings.

Do all printers connect to a parallel port?

Most printers connect to a parallel port on a computer, but some printers connect to a serial port. You can consult the printer's documentation to determine the type of port your printer uses.

Do I need to install a driver for my printer?

All printers require a driver to operate. A driver is the software that allows the computer's operating system to communicate with and control the printer. Most printers include an installation program you can use to install the necessary driver for the printer.

Printer Driver

MicroFLOPPY
Double Sided
720 k

CONSIDERATIONS

WHAT SHOULD I CONSIDER WHEN CHOOSING A PRINTER?

PRINT QUALITY

The type of printer you should choose depends on the quality of the printed pages you require. Pages produced by a low-quality printer are suitable for draft copies of documents, but documents for correspondence or business use should be printed on a higher quality printer. The cost of a printer usually increases with the quality of the printed pages it can produce.

CONSUMABLES

All printers require items that have to be replaced on a regular basis, such as ink or toner. These items are called consumables. Before you purchase a printer, you should consider the number and cost of the consumables the printer requires.

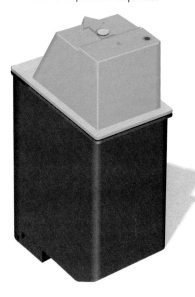

PRINT MEDIA

When choosing a printer, you should check the size and type of paper the printer accepts. If you want to print on special print media, such as envelopes, labels or transparencies, make sure the printer can accept these materials.

TYPES OF PRINTERS

WHAT TYPES OF PRINTERS ARE AVAILABLE?

DOT MATRIX PRINTER

Dot matrix printers were once very popular, but have been replaced in popularity by ink-jet printers. Inside a dot matrix printer, a print head containing small blunt pins strikes an inked ribbon to stamp images on a page. This striking action makes a dot matrix printer quite loud. Dot matrix printers typically use continuous form multipart paper and are commonly used for documents such as sales invoices and purchase orders.

LED PRINTER

Light Emitting Diode (LED) printers are similar to laser printers, but produce images on a page by using several small lights instead of a laser beam. LED printers produce pages that are comparable in quality to laser printers, but LED printers are less expensive.

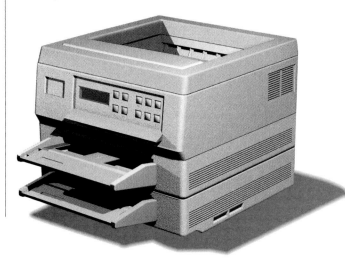

MULTIFUNCTION PRINTER

A multifunction printer can perform more than one task. This type of printer is often able to work as a fax machine, scanner and photocopier as well as a printer.

TYPES OF PRINTERS—INK-JET PRINTER

An ink-jet printer produces high-quality documents at a relatively low price. As the quality of ink-jet printers has improved, their popularity has increased. You can use the documents produced by an ink-jet printer in most circumstances, except when only the highest quality is acceptable, such as for important business correspondence.

How does an ink-jet printer work?

An ink-jet printer sprays ink through small nozzles onto a page to produce images.

Ink-jet printers use ink stored in cartridges. When the ink runs out, you replace the cartridge. You may also be able to refill a cartridge with ink. You should always use the printer manufacturer's recommended cartridges or ink for best results.

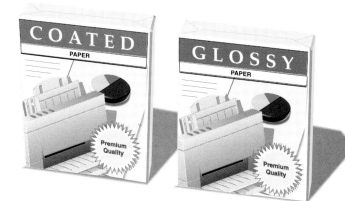

How can I improve the quality of images printed on an ink-jet printer?

Ink-jet printers can use standard paper, but image quality improves when you use more expensive, coated paper. Some ink-jet printers can also use special glossy paper to produce photographic quality images.

CONSIDERATIONS

WHAT SHOULD I CONSIDER WHEN CHOOSING AN INK-JET PRINTER?

RESOLUTION

Printer resolution is measured in dots per inch (dpi) and determines the quality of the images the printer can produce. The resolution of images produced by an ink-jet printer can range from 360 to 720 dpi.

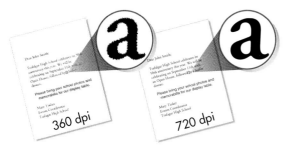

360 dpi

720 dpi

COLOR

Color ink-jet printers are very popular because they are less expensive than other types of color printers and produce high-quality images. Most color ink-jet printers spray cyan, magenta, yellow and black ink to create images on a page.

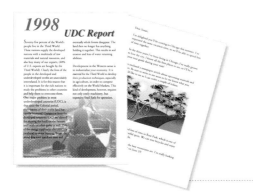

SPEED

Printer speed is measured in pages per minute (ppm) and indicates how quickly a printer can produce printed pages. Most ink-jet printers produce images at a speed of 2 to 7 ppm.

Maximum 7 ppm

SOFTWARE

Most ink-jet printers include software you can use to create special documents, such as greeting cards.

Happy Birthday

Greetings

SOFTWARE

TYPES OF PRINTERS—LASER PRINTER

A laser printer is a high-speed printer that is ideal for business documents and graphics. Laser printers produce the highest quality images, but are relatively expensive.

How does a laser printer work?

A laser printer works like a photocopier to produce high-quality images on a page. A laser beam draws images on a light-sensitive drum. The drum picks up a fine powdered ink, called toner, and then transfers the toner to the paper to create the images.

CONSIDERATIONS

WHAT SHOULD I CONSIDER WHEN CHOOSING A LASER PRINTER?

SPEED

Printer speed is measured in pages per minute (ppm) and indicates how quickly a printer can produce printed pages. Most laser printers produce images at a speed of 4 to 24 ppm.

RESOLUTION

Printer resolution is measured in dots per inch (dpi) and determines the quality of the images the printer can produce. Most laser printers can produce images at a resolution of 600 dpi.

Maximum
24 ppm

PRINT QUALITY

HOW CAN I IMPROVE THE QUALITY OF IMAGES PRINTED ON A LASER PRINTER?

TONER

Laser printers require a specific type of toner. You should check the printer's documentation to find out which type of toner the printer can use. For best results, you should not use old toner.

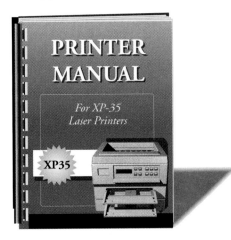

PAPER

Laser printers require a specific type of paper. For best results, check the printer's documentation to find the size, composition and weight of the paper the printer can use.

CARTRIDGES

Many small laser printers use a disposable cartridge that contains most of the components used to print, including toner. When the toner runs out, you buy a new cartridge. Using cartridges ensures that printer components are replaced on a regular basis, which can help improve print quality.

Some companies remanufacture used cartridges to produce inexpensive cartridge replacements. Using remanufactured cartridges may void your printer warranty. You should always use the printer manufacturer's recommended cartridges for best results.

MAINTAIN

How much maintenance does my printer require?

Most printers have a maintenance schedule you should follow to keep the printer in good working order. For example, most laser printers require maintenance after a certain number of pages have been printed. Certain parts of a printer must be replaced and items such as gears need to be lubricated at regular intervals.

The larger and more complex a printer is, the more maintenance the printer will require. You can consult the printer's documentation for the maintenance schedule.

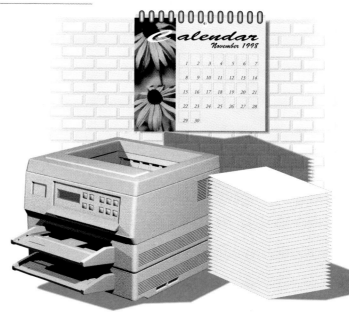

Do I need to clean my printer?

You should clean your printer on a regular basis. Over time, dust and dirt from print media can accumulate in the printer. You can use a computer vacuum cleaner or a can of compressed air to remove dust and dirt from most printers. In order to clean a large printer properly, you may need to disassemble the printer.

TROUBLESHOOT

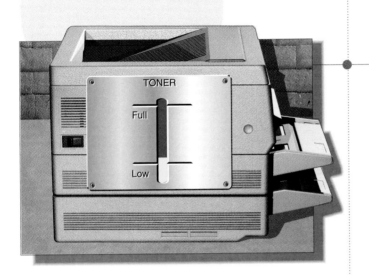

Will my printer notify me if a problem occurs?

Printers often have built-in self-diagnostic features. Some printers, such as ink-jet printers, use a series of beeps to alert you of a problem.

Most laser printers display a message that tells you a problem has occurred. A laser printer may also be able to warn you of a problem before it occurs, such as running out of toner. This gives you the opportunity to fix a problem before it happens.

Why does paper keep getting jammed in my printer?

Paper jams are the most common type of printer problem. Repeated paper jams may be caused by an obstruction in the printer, such as another sheet of paper. Paper jams may also be due to a problem with the mechanism that transfers paper through the printer. Some printers have panels you can open to access the inside of the printer and determine the cause of a paper jam.

You should be careful when pulling out paper that has become jammed. Printers contain many small sensors that may be damaged by forcibly pulling on jammed paper.

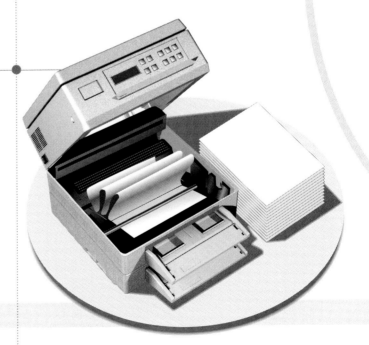

VIDEO CARD

A video card generates the text and images that appear on the display area of the monitor.

INSTALL A VIDEO CARD

Before installing a video card, turn off the computer, unplug the power cable and remove the cover from the computer case. Then ground yourself and the computer case. For information on grounding, see page 8.

Select the expansion slot on the system board where you want to install the video card.

Remove the expansion slot cover from the computer case. The cover is usually held in place by a small screw.

If necessary, use cables to connect the video card to other devices.

Place the video card in the expansion slot. Press down firmly and evenly across the top of the card until it is securely inserted in the expansion slot.

Secure the video card to the computer case using a small screw. Then replace the cover on the computer case.

SET UP AND TROUBLESHOOT

How do I set up a video card?

When you install a video card, your computer may automatically detect and set up the video card. This saves you from having to change your computer's settings so it can work with the video card. The video card may include an installation program you can use if your computer does not automatically detect and set up the video card.

What should I do if my monitor stops displaying information or no longer displays information properly?

These types of problems are often caused by the video card. To determine if your monitor is not displaying information due to a malfunctioning video card, replace the current video card with a video card you know works properly.

Some computers require that the video card be plugged into a specific expansion slot. If the monitor is not displaying information properly, check to make sure the video card is plugged into the correct expansion slot.

CONSIDERATIONS

WHAT SHOULD I CONSIDER WHEN CHOOSING A VIDEO CARD?

RESOLUTION

Resolution determines the amount of information displayed on the screen and is measured by the number of horizontal and vertical pixels. A pixel is the smallest element on the screen. Basic video cards can display a resolution of 640 x 480 or 800 x 600. Most new video cards can display a resolution of at least 1024 x 768. The video card and monitor must be able to use the same resolution.

COLOR DEPTH

The video card determines the number of colors a monitor can display. Basic video cards can display 256 colors. Today, most video cards can display over 65,000 colors.

REFRESH RATE

The refresh rate determines the speed that information is redrawn on the screen and is measured in hertz (Hz). The higher the refresh rate, the less flicker on the screen. This helps reduce eyestrain. 72 Hz is a common refresh rate. The video card and monitor must be able to use the same refresh rate.

UPGRADE

WHAT WAYS CAN I UPGRADE MY VIDEO CARD?

DRIVER

A driver is the software that allows the computer's operating system to communicate with and control the video card. All video cards require a driver. Video card drivers are frequently updated and improved. You should always ensure that you are using the correct and most up-to-date driver for your video card.

MEMORY

A video card uses memory chips to store the information it displays on the screen. You can add memory chips to a video card to increase the capabilities of the video card. Adding memory chips can increase the resolution and color depth the video card can display.

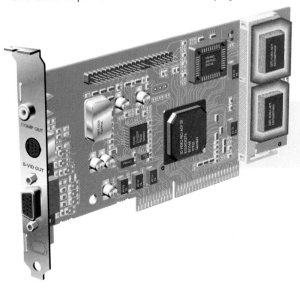

ACCELERATOR

Video cards that have a special chip, called an accelerator, can display information on the screen without using the CPU. This improves the computer's performance by freeing up the CPU for other tasks. A popular type of accelerator is the 3-D accelerator, which lets the video card display three-dimensional images faster.

MONITOR

A monitor is a device that displays text and images generated by a computer.

Before connecting a monitor, turn off the computer.

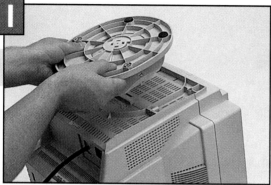

Most monitors come with a tilt-and-swivel base that lets you adjust the angle of the screen and reduce glare from overhead lighting. If necessary, attach the base to the monitor.

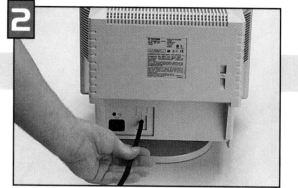

If necessary, connect the monitor cable to the back of the monitor. The monitor cable is permanently attached on some monitors.

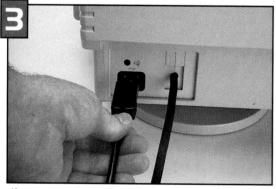

If necessary, connect the power cable to the back of the monitor. The power cable is permanently attached on some monitors.

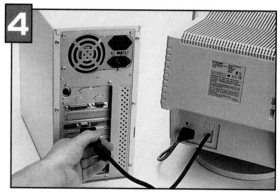

Connect the monitor cable to the monitor port at the back of the computer. The monitor port is usually located on the video card.

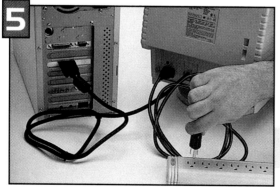

Plug the power cable from the monitor into an electrical outlet.

TYPES OF MONITORS

WHAT TYPES OF MONITORS ARE AVAILABLE?

CRT

Most monitors use Cathode Ray Tube (CRT) technology to display information. This is the same technology used in television sets. CRT technology uses a beam of high-speed electrons, called a cathode ray, to draw images on the end of a glass tube. The end of the glass tube is the screen.

LCD

Some monitors use Liquid Crystal Display (LCD) technology to display information. This is the same technology found in the displays of most digital wristwatches. The screen of an LCD monitor is made up of liquid crystal between two pieces of specially treated glass. Electrical impulses cause the liquid crystal to change color. These colors make up the images on the screen.

In the past, LCD monitors were only used on portable computers, but are now available for desktop computers. LCD monitors are more expensive than CRT monitors, but are lighter, thinner and consume less electricity. LCD monitors are also called flat-panel monitors.

CONSIDERATIONS

WHAT SHOULD I CONSIDER WHEN CHOOSING A MONITOR?

RESOLUTION

Resolution determines the amount of information a monitor can display and is measured by the number of horizontal and vertical pixels. A pixel is the smallest element on the screen. Most new monitors can display a resolution of at least 1024 x 768. The monitor and video card must be able to display the same resolution.

MULTISYNC

Some monitors can display information using only one resolution and refresh rate. A multisync monitor can display information using different resolutions and refresh rates. A multisync monitor can detect which resolution and refresh rate the video card is using and then automatically switch to the appropriate settings.

REFRESH RATE

The refresh rate is measured in hertz (Hz) and tells you the number of times per second the image on the screen is redrawn. The higher the refresh rate, the less flicker on the screen. 72 Hz is a common refresh rate. The monitor and video card must be able to use the same refresh rate.

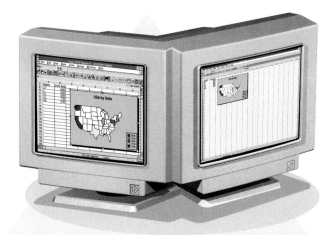

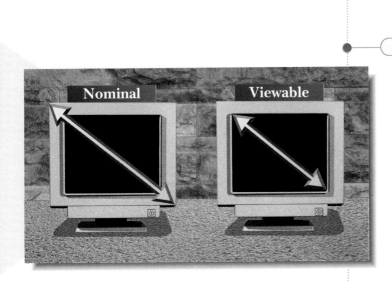

SIZE

The size of a monitor is measured two ways. The nominal size is measured diagonally across the picture tube inside the monitor. The viewable size is measured diagonally across the screen. The nominal size is usually greater than the viewable size.

Some manufacturers advertise both sizes, but many advertise only the nominal size. A common nominal monitor size is 15 inches, although 17 and 21 inch monitors are gaining in popularity as prices fall.

DOT PITCH

The dot pitch is the distance between pixels on a screen. The dot pitch determines the sharpness of images on the screen and is measured in millimeters (mm). The smaller the dot pitch, the clearer the images. For example, a monitor with a dot pitch of .26 mm will display crisper images than a monitor with a dot pitch of .30 mm.

NON-INTERLACED

A non-interlaced monitor greatly reduces screen flicker. Non-interlaced monitors are more expensive than old, interlaced monitors, but help reduce eyestrain.

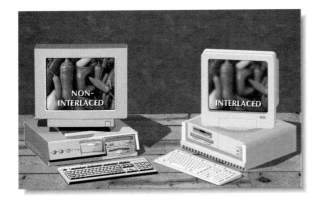

TROUBLESHOOT AND MAINTAIN

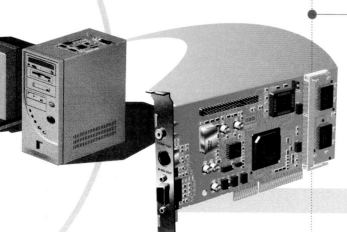

Why is my monitor not working properly?

Monitors tend to be one of the most reliable and robust components of a computer system. When a monitor fails to display information properly or does not display any information at all, the problem usually lies with the video card. A video card translates instructions from the computer to a form the monitor can understand. For information about troubleshooting a video card, see page 75.

Why are the images on my screen discolored?

If images on your screen seem to display a blue, green or purple tinge, one of the primary colors may be missing. The cause of the problem may be a loose connection between the monitor and the video card. The end of the cable that connects the monitor to the video card has a connector with two screws. Both of these screws should be fastened to the video card to ensure a secure connection.

Why is there a dark area on my screen?

Monitors are susceptible to interference from the magnetic fields generated by a device such as a heater. If a monitor displays a dark or discolored area on the screen, it may have been exposed to strong magnetic fields.

You should remove any magnetic devices from the area where the monitor is located and then degauss the screen to demagnetize it. Many monitors degauss automatically each time they are turned on. Some monitors also have a degauss button you can use.

How do I clean my monitor?

Before cleaning a monitor, you should refer to the monitor's documentation for instructions. Many monitors have an anti-glare coating that helps to reduce the amount of light reflected off the screen. Some monitors also have an anti-static coating that repels dust. If you use the wrong substance to clean the screen, these coatings may be affected.

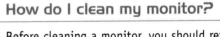

TV TUNER CARD

A TV tuner card allows you to watch television programs on your computer.

Before installing a TV tuner card, turn off the computer, unplug the power cable and remove the cover from the computer case. Then ground yourself and the computer case. For information on grounding, see page 8.

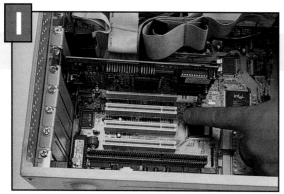

Select the expansion slot on the system board where you want to install the TV tuner card.

Remove the expansion slot cover from the computer case. The cover is usually held in place by a small screw.

If necessary, use a cable to connect the TV tuner card to other devices.

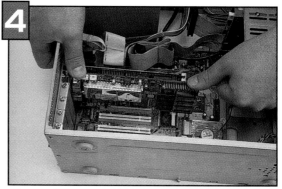

Place the TV tuner card in the expansion slot. Press down firmly and evenly across the top of the card until it is securely inserted in the expansion slot.

Secure the TV tuner card to the computer case using a small screw. Then replace the cover on the computer case.

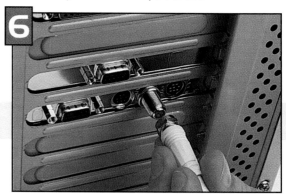

Connect the television cable to the TV tuner card.

SET UP

Does my TV tuner card come with an installation program?

Every TV tuner card comes with an installation program you can use to set up the TV tuner card to work with the computer.

CONSIDERATIONS

What should I consider when choosing a TV tuner card?

VIDEO CAPTURE

Most TV tuner cards allow you to save still images and full-motion video clips from a television program as a file on your hard drive.

INTERCAST TECHNOLOGY

Some television channels use Intercast technology to broadcast additional information with their programs. This allows you to watch a television program and view text and graphics related to the program at the same time. Most TV tuner cards support Intercast technology.

CLOSED CAPTIONING

Most TV tuner cards can scan the closed captioning text of a television channel for a keyword. When the keyword appears, the TV tuner card displays the television program on your monitor.

SOUND CARD

A sound card allows a computer to play and record high-quality sound.

INSTALL A SOUND CARD

Before installing a sound card, turn off the computer, unplug the power cable and remove the cover from the computer case. Then ground yourself and the computer case. For information on grounding, see page 8.

1 Select the expansion slot on the system board where you want to install the sound card.

2 Remove the expansion slot cover from the computer case. The cover is usually held in place by a small screw.

3 If necessary, use the jumpers or switches on the sound card to adjust the settings for the sound card.

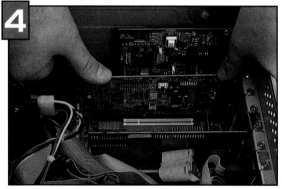

4 Place the sound card in the expansion slot. Press down firmly and evenly across the top of the card until it is securely inserted in the expansion slot.

5 Secure the sound card to the computer case using a small screw. Then replace the cover on the computer case.

SET UP

Do I need to adjust the settings for my sound card?

Sound cards require several computer resources, such as Interrupt Requests (IRQ), Direct Memory Access (DMA) channels and Input/Output (I/O) addresses. You can consult the documentation included with your sound card for information on the resource settings the sound card requires.

Before installing a sound card, make sure you have a list of the resources used by the other devices. If the sound card requires the same resources as another device, you may need to change the settings for the device. For more information on resource settings, see page 164.

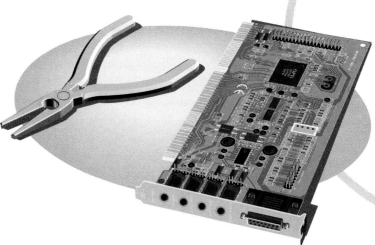

Do I need to install a driver for my sound card?

Sound cards require one or more drivers. A driver is the software that allows the computer's operating system to communicate with and control the sound card. Most sound cards include an installation program that installs all the necessary drivers at once. If there is no installation program, you may have to install a separate driver for each port and jack on the sound card. Drivers are usually available at the sound card manufacturer's Web site.

CONSIDERATIONS

WHAT SHOULD I CONSIDER WHEN CHOOSING A SOUND CARD?

MIDI SUPPORT

Musical Instrument Digital Interface (MIDI) is a set of instructions that allows you to connect a musical instrument, such as a synthesizer, to a sound card. This lets you use a computer to play, record and edit music. Many musicians use MIDI to compose music on a computer.

A sound card that supports MIDI also ensures that a computer can generate the sounds often found in games and presentation packages.

FM AND WAVETABLE SYNTHESIS

There are two ways a sound card can produce MIDI sound—FM synthesis and Wavetable synthesis. FM synthesis uses mathematical formulas to imitate the sounds of musical instruments. This results in less realistic sound.

Wavetable synthesis uses actual recordings of musical instruments. This results in rich, realistic sound. Sound cards that use Wavetable synthesis are more expensive, but produce higher quality sound than cards that use FM synthesis.

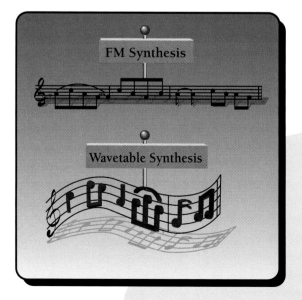

SOUND BLASTER COMPATIBLE

Sound Blaster is the accepted industry standard for sound cards. You should purchase a Sound Blaster compatible sound card to ensure that the sound card will work with most programs and operating systems.

SAMPLING SIZE AND RATE

The sampling size and rate of a sound card determines the quality of the sound produced. For good quality sound, buy a sound card with at least a 16-bit sampling size and a 44.1 KHz sampling rate.

Sampling Size:
16-bit
Sampling Rate:
44.1 KHz

UPGRADE

Can I upgrade my sound card?

You may be able to add memory to your sound card. Adding memory allows you to increase the capabilities of the sound card. Sound cards usually contain more than enough memory for most programs, including games. In most cases, you will only need to add memory if you plan to use the computer to compose or sample music.

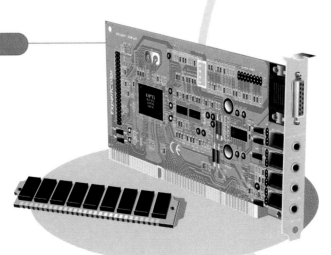

Speakers allow you to hear the sound generated by a sound card.

Most computers come equipped with low-quality speakers. You may want to upgrade to higher quality speakers if you use your computer to play games or listen to music CDs.

CONNECT A SET OF SPEAKERS

Before connecting a set of speakers, turn off the computer.

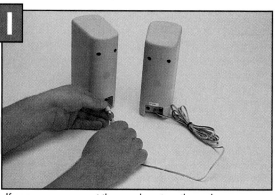

If necessary, connect the speakers together using the speaker cable.

Position the speakers in the desired location.

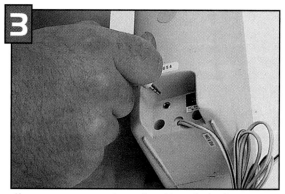

If necessary, connect the audio cable to the back of the main speaker. The main speaker often has a volume control and power switch.

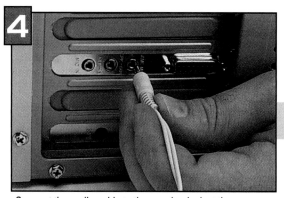

Connect the audio cable to the speaker jack at the back of the computer. The speaker jack is usually found on the sound card.

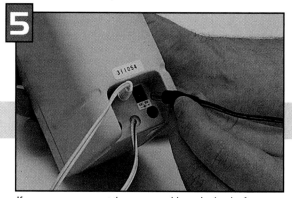

If necessary, connect the power cable to the back of the main speaker. Then plug the power cable into an electrical outlet.

CONSIDERATIONS

WHAT SHOULD I CONSIDER WHEN CHOOSING SPEAKERS?

SHIELDED SPEAKERS

When choosing speakers, make sure you select shielded speakers. Shielded speakers prevent the magnets inside the speakers from distorting the images on a monitor or damaging hard drives, floppy disks and tape cartridges.

FREQUENCY

Frequency is measured in hertz (Hz) and refers to the range of high and low sounds speakers can produce. The range of human hearing is 20 to 20,000 Hz. Some high-quality speakers have a frequency of 40 to 20,000 Hz.

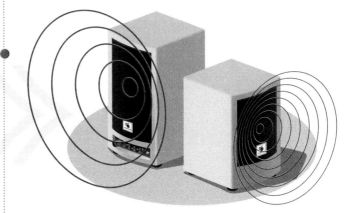

FEATURES

Some speakers include features that can enhance the quality of sound the speakers produce. For example, a built-in amplifier can strengthen the signal from the sound card to improve speaker performance. Speakers that include 3-D sound enhancement technology seem to produce sound from a wider area. Some speaker systems also include a subwoofer, which produces low-frequency sounds and gives speakers a richer sound.

MICROPHONE

CONNECT A MICROPHONE

You can use a microphone to record speech and other sounds.

Before connecting a microphone, turn off the computer.

1

Some microphones come with a stand that lets you adjust the angle of the microphone to improve recording quality. If necessary, attach the stand to the microphone.

Position the microphone where you can use it comfortably.

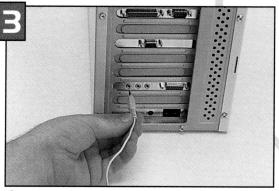

Connect the cable from the microphone to the microphone jack at the back of the computer. The microphone jack is usually located on the sound card.

PROGRAMS

What types of programs can I use my microphone with?

You can use a microphone with some types of conferencing programs to communicate with others over the Internet. With voice control programs, you can speak into a microphone and use voice commands to control your computer. Speech recognition programs allow you to speak into a microphone to create documents, instead of typing text with your keyboard.

CONSIDERATIONS

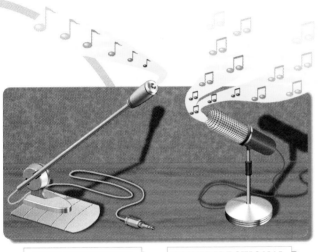

UNIDIRECTIONAL   OMNIDIRECTIONAL

What type of microphone should I choose?

The type of microphone you should choose depends on the way you want the microphone to record sound. A unidirectional microphone records sound from one direction, which helps reduce the amount of background noise that is recorded. This type of microphone is useful for recording an individual voice.

An omnidirectional microphone records sound from all directions. This type of microphone is useful for recording several voices in a group conversation.

TROUBLESHOOT

How can I improve the quality of my recordings?

Make sure the microphone is positioned away from sources of unwanted background noise, such as appliances or open windows. You should also make sure the microphone is positioned close to, but not directly in front of, the person using the microphone.

If changing the position of the microphone does not improve the quality of your recordings, you may have to change the microphone's settings. Some operating systems, including Windows 95 and Windows 98, allow you to adjust the balance and volume settings for the microphone.

JOYSTICK

A joystick is a device that allows you to interact with a computer game.

CONNECT A JOYSTICK

Before connecting a joystick, turn off the computer.

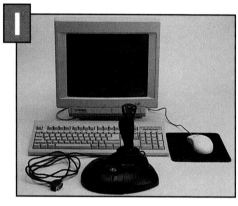

1

Position the joystick where you can use it comfortably. Most joysticks have suction cups that allow you to secure the joystick to your desk.

2

Connect the cable from the joystick to the joystick port at the back of the computer. The joystick port is usually located on the sound card.

UPGRADE

What kind of joystick can I upgrade to?

ENHANCED JOYSTICKS

Some enhanced joysticks have extra controls to improve the way you play games. For example, enhanced joysticks designed specifically for driving games include a steering wheel and pedals. Other enhanced joysticks are programmed to move in response to actions in a game.

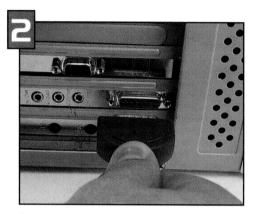

GAMEPAD

A gamepad is a small, handheld device that typically consists of a movement control on the left and function buttons on the right. Gamepads are useful for games that require rapid movement, such as fighting games.

SET UP

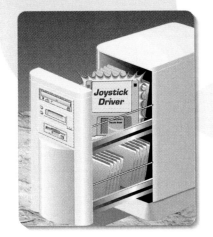

Do I need to install a driver for my joystick?

If you want to use your joystick to play a game designed for Windows 95 or Windows 98, you may need to install a joystick driver included with Windows. You can consult your joystick's documentation to determine which driver you should install.

How do I adjust my joystick's settings?

You can calibrate your joystick to adjust and fine-tune the joystick's settings. Some joysticks have trim wheels you can use to help calibrate the joystick. You can also use an operating system such as Windows 95 or Windows 98 to calibrate your joystick. Some joysticks, such as enhanced joysticks, may need to be calibrated using the software that came with the joystick.

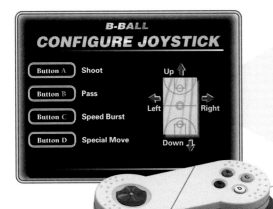

Do I need to set up my joystick to work with a specific game?

Some games require you to set up the joystick within the game. For example, you may need to specify the type of joystick you are using or assign specific functions to the buttons on the joystick. You can follow the directions in the game to set up the joystick.

SCANNER

A scanner is a device that reads graphics and paper documents such as letters, forms and news clippings into a computer.

Before connecting a scanner, turn off the computer.

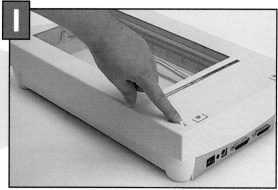

Many scanners have a transit lock, which secures the scanner's internal components during shipping. If necessary, release the transit lock.

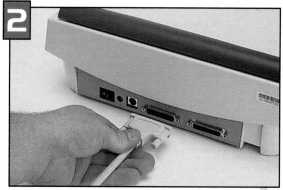

Connect the scanner cable to the port at the back of the scanner.

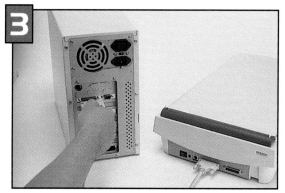

Connect the scanner cable to a parallel port at the back of the computer. Some scanners connect to a SCSI port instead of a parallel port.

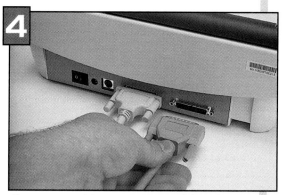

If you connected the scanner to a parallel port in step 3, you can connect the cable from your printer to the printer port at the back of the scanner.

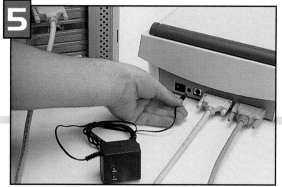

Connect the power cable to the power connector at the back of the scanner. Then plug the power cable into an electrical outlet.

TYPES OF SCANNERS

WHAT TYPES OF SCANNERS ARE AVAILABLE?

FLATBED

A flatbed scanner can scan single sheets of paper and pages in a book. Most flatbed scanners can scan documents up to 8.5 inches wide and 11 inches long. Some flatbed scanners can scan documents up to 8.5 inches wide and 14 inches long.

SHEET-FED

A sheet-fed scanner can scan only single sheets of paper. If you want to scan a page in a book, you have to tear out the page.

Sheet-fed scanners are less expensive and more compact than flatbed scanners, but produce lower quality images.

HANDHELD

A handheld scanner can scan images up to four inches wide. You must manually move the scanner over the image you want to scan. This movement usually affects the quality of the scanned image.

Handheld scanners are inexpensive and portable, but the popularity of handheld scanners has decreased as the prices of flatbed and sheet-fed scanners have fallen.

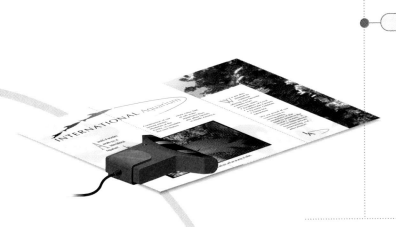

CONSIDERATIONS

WHAT SHOULD I CONSIDER WHEN CHOOSING A SCANNER?

RESOLUTION

The resolution of a scanner determines the amount of detail the scanner can detect. Scanner resolution is measured in dots per inch (dpi). Most scanners can detect 300 x 600 dpi, but some scanners can detect up to 2400 x 1200 dpi.

TWAIN COMPATIBLE

All scanners include a driver that allows the operating system and programs, such as image editing software, to work with the scanner. TWAIN is the accepted industry standard for scanner drivers. A scanner that uses a TWAIN driver can be used by most operating systems and programs.

COLOR DEPTH

The color depth of a scanner is measured in bits and indicates the number of colors the scanner can detect. The more colors the scanner can detect, the higher the quality of the scan. Most scanners have a 24-bit color depth. A 24-bit scanner is capable of detecting over 16 million different colors.

SOFTWARE

WHAT TYPES OF SOFTWARE COME WITH A SCANNER?

IMAGE EDITING SOFTWARE

Image editing software allows you to change the appearance of a scanned graphic. You can adjust the brightness, contrast and color balance of a graphic. You can also make major changes to a graphic, such as removing an object. The image editing software included with most scanners is a limited version of commercial image editing software.

OCR SOFTWARE

Optical Character Recognition (OCR) software places scanned text into a document that can be edited in a word processor. The OCR software included with most scanners is a limited version of commercial OCR software.

TROUBLESHOOT

Why is my scanner not working properly?

In most cases, if your scanner does not work properly, the cause of the problem is an incorrectly installed driver or software program. You should try re-installing the driver or software to correct the problem.

If the problem persists, the scanner may have a hardware malfunction and may need to be returned to the manufacturer.

DIGITAL CAMERA

A digital camera lets you take photos that you can view and print using a computer.

Most digital cameras include a color Liquid Crystal Display (LCD) screen, which you can use to preview your shots and view photos you have taken.

HOW DO I TRANSFER PHOTOS FROM MY DIGITAL CAMERA TO A COMPUTER?

Digital cameras include a cable that allows you to connect the camera to a port on the computer. This connection allows you to transfer the photos from the camera to the computer.

TROUBLESHOOT

My digital camera is not working properly. What should I do?

All digital cameras use batteries for power. If your digital camera is having problems such as a malfunctioning flash or is producing distorted images, you should check to see if the batteries in the camera are low on power. For best results, you should use fully charged batteries each time you begin using your digital camera.

If problems persist, you may need to return the digital camera to the manufacturer for repair.

CONSIDERATIONS

What should I consider when choosing a digital camera?

640 x 480

1,152 x 864

RESOLUTION

The resolution of a digital camera determines the quality of photos the camera can produce. A digital camera with a resolution of 640 x 480 can produce photos suitable for viewing on a monitor. Digital cameras with a resolution of 1,152 x 864 or higher, called megapixel cameras, are best if you want to print good quality photos.

MEMORY

Digital cameras store photos in memory until you transfer the photos to a computer. Most digital cameras have either built-in or removable memory, but some cameras have both.

Removable

Most digital cameras with removable memory store photos on a memory card. Some digital cameras store photos on a regular floppy disk that fits inside the camera. You can replace a memory card or floppy disk when it is full.

Built-in

The built-in memory in most digital cameras can store at least 20 photos. Once the built-in memory is full, you must transfer the photos to a computer before taking more photos.

The Universal Serial Bus (USB) hub allows you to connect multiple devices to your computer.

CONNECT A USB HUB

Before connecting a USB hub, turn on the computer.

Connect the USB cable to the computer port on the USB hub.

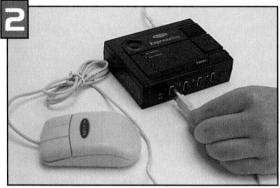

Connect your USB devices to the device ports on the USB hub.

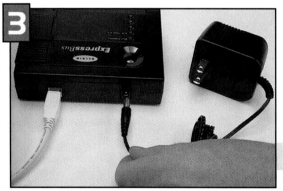

If necessary, connect the power cable to the USB hub. Then plug the power cable into an electrical outlet.

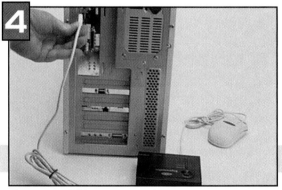

Connect the USB cable to the USB port at the back of the computer.

USB PORT

I want to use a USB hub, but my computer does not have a USB port. What should I do?

You can add a USB port to your computer by installing a USB expansion card. To install an expansion card, perform steps 4 to 6 on page 54.

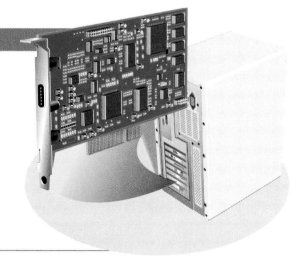

SET UP

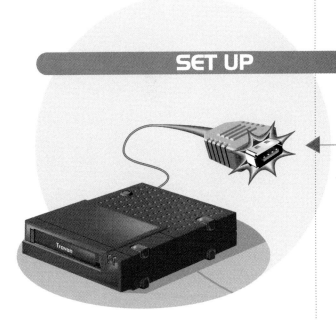

Which devices can I connect to a USB hub?

You can only connect devices that have a USB connector to a USB hub. Since USB is a new technology, there is not currently a wide range of devices with USB connectors. Eventually many devices will have USB connectors, including tape drives, printers, modems and scanners.

How many devices can a USB hub support?

You can plug up to four devices into a USB hub, but a USB port on a computer can support up to 127 devices. To connect more devices to the computer, you can attach, or daisy chain, several hubs together. You can also purchase a USB device, such as a monitor, that has a built-in hub.

Do I have to change the computer's settings when I connect a device to my USB hub?

When you connect a device, the USB hub automatically detects the device and adjusts the computer's settings to work with the device. You do not have to restart the computer.

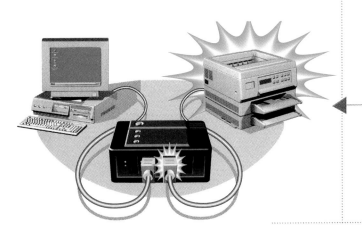

UPS

An Uninterruptible Power Supply (UPS) is a device that can condition incoming power to prevent power fluctuations, such as spikes and surges, from reaching your computer. In the event of a power failure, most UPSs can also provide 5 to 20 minutes of power.

CONNECT A UPS

Before connecting a UPS, turn off the computer and monitor.

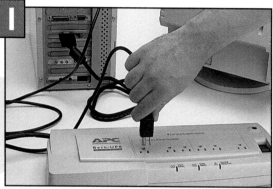

Unplug the computer's power cable from the electrical outlet and plug it into the outlet on the UPS.

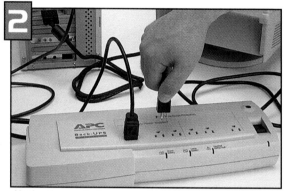

Unplug the monitor's power cable from the electrical outlet and plug it into the outlet on the UPS.

Plug the power cable from the UPS into an electrical outlet.

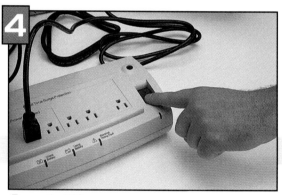

Turn on the UPS.

Will my UPS work as soon as I connect it?

A battery inside a UPS stores electrical power. The battery in most UPSs requires 24 hours to charge completely. You do not have to wait for the battery to finish charging to use the computer, but the UPS will not work properly until the battery is completely charged.

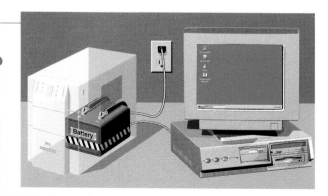

TYPES OF UPSs

WHAT TYPES OF UPSs ARE AVAILABLE?

STANDBY

A standby UPS switches to battery power when it detects a power failure. There is usually a brief delay before the battery begins supplying power. Some standby UPSs also offer power conditioning features. This type of UPS is typically the least expensive.

LINE-INTERACTIVE

A line-interactive UPS contains a transformer that continuously conditions the incoming power. This type of UPS only switches to battery power when the power level falls very low, such as when a power failure occurs.

ONLINE

An online UPS constantly uses the battery to condition the incoming power and therefore does not have to switch in the event of a power failure. This type of UPS provides the most protection from power fluctuations and is generally the most expensive.

CONSIDERATIONS

WHAT SHOULD I CONSIDER WHEN CHOOSING A UPS?

VA RATING

The VA rating determines how much power a UPS can deliver. The higher the VA rating, the more devices the UPS can support and the longer the battery can provide temporary power. A UPS with a 250 to 400 VA rating is sufficient for most home computers.

TELEPHONE SOCKET

Many UPSs have a telephone socket where you can plug in the telephone cable from a modem. This protects the modem and computer from power surges transmitted over telephone lines.

AUTOMATIC SHUTDOWN

Some UPSs include software that can automatically close programs and shut down a computer in the event of a power failure. This is useful if you are not at the computer when the power fails.

WARNING!

Power failure detected.
Shutting down in 5 minutes...

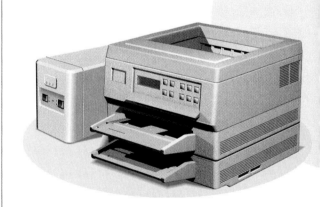

LARGE DEVICES

Most UPSs are not designed to support devices that require a lot of power to operate, such as a photocopier or laser printer. You should only plug these devices into a UPS specially designed for large devices.

TROUBLESHOOT AND MAINTAIN

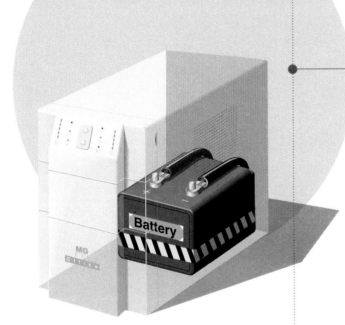

How can I tell if the battery needs to be replaced in my UPS?

UPSs tend to be very reliable and usually work for about 4 years before you need to replace the battery. Problems associated with a faulty battery can include computer lockups, device failures and unexpected computer shutdowns.

Before replacing a battery, you should make sure the battery is the cause of the problems you are experiencing. Disconnect the computer from any devices, such as a printer, which are plugged into an electrical outlet on the wall. If the problems stop, the cause may have been power from an electrical outlet not protected by the UPS. If the problems persist, the battery is likely the cause.

Should I test my UPS?

You should regularly test your UPS to make sure it is working properly. Many UPSs have a test button you can use to test the status of the UPS. You can also unplug your UPS from the electrical outlet on the wall to ensure the UPS is capable of providing temporary power if a power failure occurs.

CHAPTER 4

COMMUNICATION DEVICES

Communication devices allow you to send and receive information. This chapter explains how network interface cards and modems help your computer transmit information.

NETWORK INTERFACE CARD

A Network Interface Card (NIC) physically connects a computer to a network and controls the flow of information between the computer and the network.

INSTALL A NETWORK INTERFACE CARD

Before installing a network interface card, turn off the computer, unplug the power cable and remove the cover from the computer case. Then ground yourself and the computer case. For information on grounding, see page 8.

Remove the cover for the expansion slot where you want to install the card. The cover is usually held in place by a small screw.

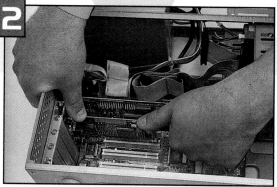

Place the network interface card in the expansion slot. Press down firmly and evenly across the top of the card until it is securely inserted.

Secure the network interface card to the computer case using a small screw. Then replace the cover on the computer case.

Plug the network cable into the network interface card at the back of the computer.

SET UP

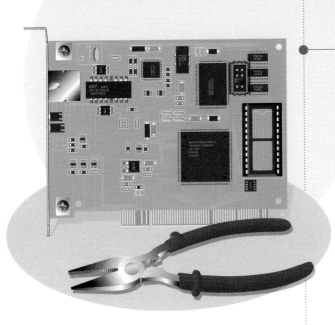

Do I need to adjust the jumpers on my network interface card?

If your network interface card requires the same computer resources as another device, such as Interrupt Request (IRQ) settings, you may need to change the settings for the card. You may also need to change the settings for the card to specify which type of cable you are using.

Some network interface cards require you to use jumpers to adjust these settings, but most new network interface cards include an installation program you can use. Consult the card's documentation for information on how to change the settings.

Do I need to install a driver for my network interface card?

Network interface cards come with drivers for different types of operating systems. A driver is the software that allows the computer's operating system to communicate with and control the network interface card. To ensure the network interface card performs at its best, you must install the correct driver.

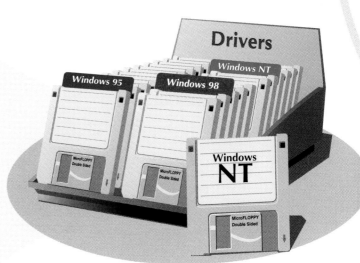

CONSIDERATIONS

**WHAT
SHOULD
I CONSIDER
WHEN CHOOSING
A NETWORK
INTERFACE
CARD?**

NETWORK TYPE

The most popular type of network is Ethernet. Other common types of networks include Token Ring and ARCnet. A network interface card designed for one type of network cannot be used on another type of network.

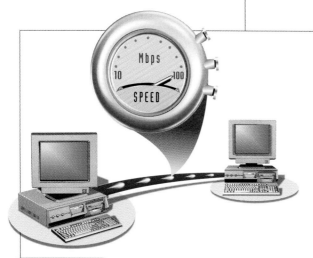

SPEED

The speed of a network is measured in megabits per second (Mbps) and indicates how fast information can transfer. Most Ethernet networks can transfer information at 10 Mbps, although some Ethernet networks can transfer information at 100 Mbps. New Ethernet network interface cards can transfer information at both 10 and 100 Mbps.

CABLE

The two most popular types of network cable are coaxial and twisted pair. Coaxial cable, which is similar to television cable, is inexpensive and easy to work with. Twisted pair cable is similar to telephone cable and is less expensive than coaxial cable.

The network interface card you choose must be compatible with the type of cable you want to use. Some network interface cards have two ports, allowing you to use either type of cable.

COAXIAL

TWISTED PAIR

TEST AND TROUBLESHOOT

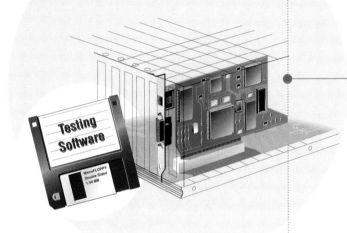

How can I test my network interface card?

Many network interface cards include testing software you can use to verify that the card is set up correctly and the computer can communicate with the card. Some testing software also lets you test the communication between your computer and other computers on the network.

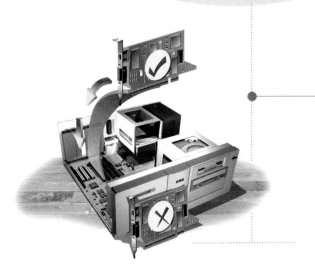

Why am I having problems accessing the network?

If you are experiencing problems transferring information on the network or cannot access the network, the cable is usually the cause. To verify that a cable is the cause of a problem, replace the current cable with a cable you know works properly.

I think my network interface card is malfunctioning. How can I confirm this?

A malfunctioning network interface card can cause computer problems and prevent you from accessing the network. You can easily confirm if a network interface card is malfunctioning by replacing the current network interface card with a card you know works properly.

MODEM

A modem is a device that lets computers exchange information through telephone lines.

Before installing a modem, turn off the computer.

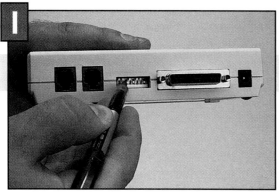

If necessary, use the switches on the back or bottom of the modem to adjust the settings for the modem. Consult the modem's documentation to determine if you need to adjust the settings.

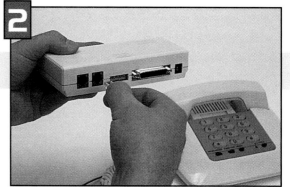

If desired, connect the cable from your telephone to the back of the modem.

Connect the telephone line to the back of the modem. Then connect the telephone line to the telephone jack on the wall.

Connect the serial cable to the back of the modem. Then connect the serial cable to a serial port at the back of the computer.

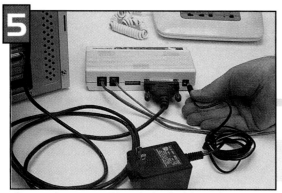

Connect the power cable to the back of the modem. Then plug the power cable into an electrical outlet.

INSTALL AN INTERNAL MODEM

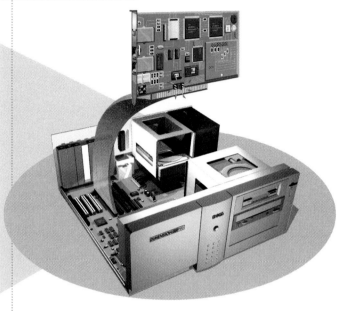

An internal modem is a circuit board that plugs into an expansion slot inside a computer. You can install an internal modem the same way you install an expansion card. To install an expansion card, perform steps 4 to 6 on page 54.

You may have to adjust the jumpers on an internal modem so the modem can work with the computer. When you install an internal modem, your computer thinks another serial port has been added. If you want the modem to use one of the existing serial ports, you must adjust the jumpers on the modem. To avoid conflicts, you must then change the computer's settings to disable the existing serial port. For information on computer settings, see page 168.

SET UP

Setting up new modem...

Will my computer automatically detect the modem?

When you install an external or internal modem, the computer may automatically detect and set up the modem, installing the necessary driver for you. If the computer does not automatically set up the modem and install the driver, you will need to install the driver included with the modem.

CONSIDERATIONS

MODEM TYPE

WHAT SHOULD I CONSIDER WHEN CHOOSING A MODEM?

When choosing a modem, you should consider the type of modem that best suits your needs. An external modem is portable and easy to install, but is usually more expensive than an internal modem. Internal modems are more complicated to install, but are usually less expensive than external modems.

FAX

Most modems can send and receive faxes. You can create a document on your computer and then fax the document to another computer or fax machine.

VOICE

Some modems have voice capabilities that allow you to use the modem to send and receive voice telephone calls. This lets you use the modem as a hands-free telephone. You may also be able to use a modem with voice capabilities as an answering machine for voice telephone messages.

SPEED

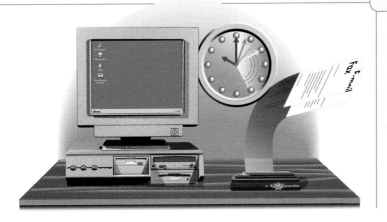

The speed of a modem is measured in kilobits per second (Kbps) and indicates the amount of information the modem can send and receive. Most modems can send and receive information at 33.6 Kbps. Some new modems can receive information at 56 Kbps, but can send information at only 33.6 Kbps.

UPGRADE

ADDITIONAL CAPABILITIES

WHAT SHOULD I CONSIDER WHEN UPGRADING A MODEM?

You may be able to upgrade your current modem to add capabilities, such as a faster speed, that were not available when the modem was produced. An upgrade may be a program you install on the computer to upgrade the modem automatically or a chip you add to the modem. You may have to return some modems to the manufacturer to be upgraded.

COMMUNICATIONS PROGRAM

A communications program is software that manages the transmission of information between two modems. A communications program usually comes packaged with a modem. When upgrading to a new modem, you should consider the features that the communications program included with the modem offers.

TEST AND TROUBLESHOOT

Can I test the modem to make sure it is communicating properly with my computer?

Once a modem is installed and set up, you can use a program such as Phone Dialer to test the modem. Phone Dialer is a program included with Windows 95 and Windows 98 that allows you to use your modem and telephone to make telephone calls. To test the modem, use Phone Dialer to try to make a telephone call. If the modem and computer are communicating properly, the modem will make a noise.

Why is my modem performing poorly?

When a computer automatically detects a modem, the computer may install the wrong driver. While a modem can operate with the wrong driver, modem performance is best when the correct driver is installed. You should always ensure you are using the correct and most up-to-date driver for your modem. The latest drivers are usually available at the modem manufacturer's Web site.

Why is my modem having problems establishing a connection?

If your modem has trouble establishing a connection or staying connected, the problem may be due to the features on your telephone line, such as voice-mail or call waiting. The voice-mail feature changes the tone of the telephone line to indicate a message is waiting. This change in tone may prevent the modem from establishing a connection.

The call waiting feature generates a beep to indicate an incoming call. This beep may cause some modems to lose the connection. You should disable the call waiting feature before using a modem.

My modem is operating slowly. What is wrong?

If the speed at which your modem transfers information seems slow, the problem may be with the quality of the telephone line. For example, a modem with a speed of 33.6 Kbps may not reach that speed if the telephone line quality is poor. If you frequently get slow transfer speeds, you should contact your local telephone company.

CABLE MODEM

A cable modem is a device that lets computers access the Internet using television cable.

Most cable companies will install and set up a cable modem for you.

CONNECT A CABLE MODEM

To connect a cable modem, you must first install a network interface card. To install a network interface card, see page 110. Before connecting the cable modem, turn off the computer.

Connect the television cable to the back of the cable modem.

Connect the network cable to the back of the cable modem.

Connect the network cable to the network interface card at the back of the computer.

Attach the power cable to the back of the cable modem. Then plug the cable into an electrical outlet.

SET UP

Do I have to set up my computer to use a cable modem?

Before you can use a cable modem, you must adjust your computer's settings so the computer can work on a network. Most operating systems include software you can use to adjust your computer's settings to work on a network. The cable modem will include any additional software you need.

BENEFITS

What are the benefits of using a cable modem instead of a telephone modem?

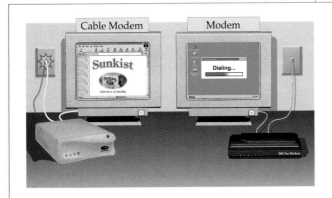

SPEED

Television cable can transfer information much faster than telephone lines. Therefore, most cable modems are capable of transferring information at much greater speeds than telephone modems.

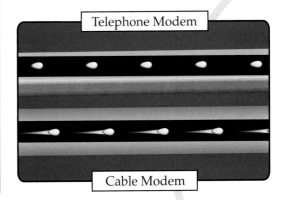

CONVENIENCE

Using a cable modem to access the Internet is more convenient than using a telephone modem. A cable modem supplies a permanent connection to the Internet so you do not have to dial into an Internet service provider each time you want to access the Internet. Also, a cable modem does not tie up your phone line the way a telephone modem does when you are accessing the Internet.

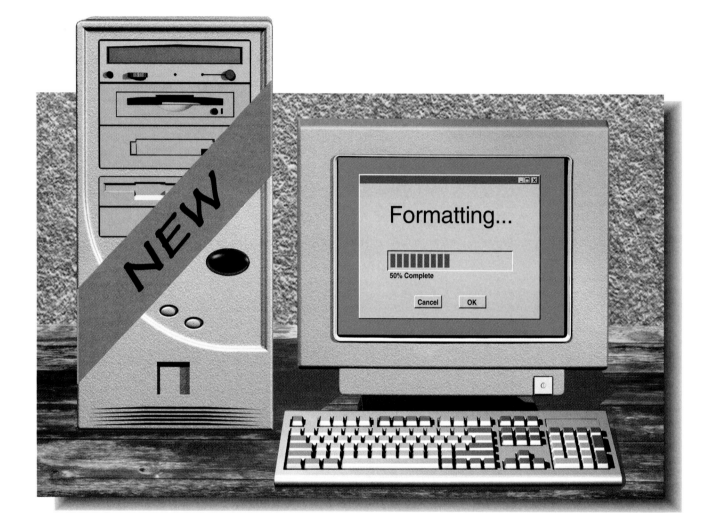

CHAPTER 5

STORAGE DEVICES

A storage device reads and records information on storage media. This chapter discusses hard and floppy drives, removable devices and more.

HARD DRIVE

REPLACE A HARD DRIVE

A hard drive is the primary device that a computer uses to store data.

Before replacing a hard drive, turn off the computer, unplug the power cable and remove the cover from the computer case. Then ground yourself and the computer case. For information on grounding, see page 8.

Remove the screws that secure the hard drive in the drive bay.

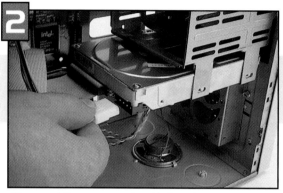

Disconnect the power supply cable from the back of the hard drive.

Disconnect the ribbon cable from the back of the hard drive. Then slide the drive out of the drive bay.

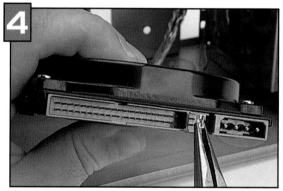

If necessary, adjust the jumpers on the new hard drive. Then slide the drive into the drive bay.

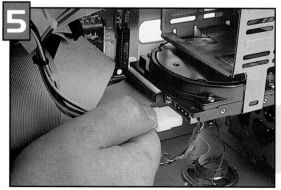

Connect the power supply cable and the ribbon cable to the back of the hard drive.

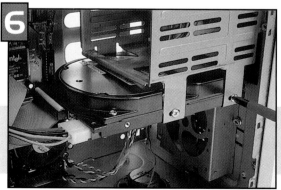

Using small screws, secure the hard drive in the drive bay. Then replace the cover on the computer case.

SET UP

Do I need to adjust the jumpers on my new hard drive?

If you use an Enhanced Integrated Drive Electronics (EIDE) ribbon cable to connect the hard drive and another device to the computer, you may have to change the jumpers on the devices. One device must be set as the master, while the other is set as the slave.

You may also need to adjust the jumpers on the hard drive if you are using a Small Computer System Interface (SCSI) ribbon cable to connect multiple devices. Each device must be assigned a unique number from zero to seven.

Consult the drive's documentation for information on adjusting the jumpers.

Will my computer automatically detect the hard drive?

Your computer may automatically detect and set up a hard drive you install. If your computer does not set up the hard drive, you may need to change the computer's settings so it can work with the drive. For information on computer settings, see page 168.

New Hard Drive Detected

HARD DRIVE

INSIDE A HARD DRIVE

How does a hard drive work?

A hard drive magnetically stores data on a stack of disks, called platters. The disks spin at a high speed inside the drive. The drive has several read/write heads that move across the spinning disks to read and record data.

CONSIDERATIONS

WHAT SHOULD I CONSIDER WHEN CHOOSING A HARD DRIVE?

CAPACITY

Compared to other storage media, such as floppy disks, hard drives can store a large amount of data. The amount of data a hard drive can store is measured in bytes. A hard drive with a capacity of 3 to 10 GB will suit most home and business users. You can add additional storage to a computer by replacing an existing hard drive with a larger one or installing an additional hard drive. Purchase the largest hard drive you can afford, since programs and data will quickly fill a hard drive.

HARD DRIVE

INDY Racing

AVERAGE ACCESS TIME

The average access time is the speed at which a hard drive finds data and is measured in milliseconds (ms). One millisecond equals 1/1000 of a second. Most hard drives have an average access time of 8 to 15 ms. The lower the average access time, the faster the hard drive.

UDMA

Hard drives that use Ultra Direct Memory Access (UDMA) technology can transfer data to and from a computer faster. To take advantage of the faster speed of a UDMA hard drive, your computer must also use UDMA technology. UDMA is also known as Ultra ATA.

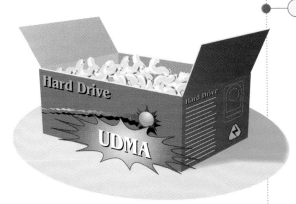

EXTERNAL HARD DRIVE

A hard drive is usually located inside the computer case. Some hard drives, however, are located outside the computer case. An external hard drive sits on your desk and plugs into the back of your computer. When an external hard drive malfunctions or needs to be upgraded, it is very easy to replace. An external hard drive can also easily be transported to another computer.

FORMAT A HARD DRIVE

Your hard drive must be formatted before you can use the drive to store data. Formatting a hard drive involves three steps.

IS THERE ANYTHING THAT MUST BE DONE BEFORE I CAN USE MY HARD DRIVE TO STORE DATA?

NEW

Formatting...

50% Complete

Cancel   OK

LOW-LEVEL FORMAT

The low-level format is the first step in formatting a hard drive. The manufacturer of the hard drive performs a low-level format when the hard drive is produced.

During a low-level format, the surface of each disk in the hard drive is divided into circles, called tracks. The tracks are then divided into sections, called sectors. The hard drive will store data on the tracks and sectors.

A low-level format also marks any tracks that cannot store data. The hard drive will not attempt to store data on bad tracks. It is normal for a hard drive to have some bad tracks.

PARTITIONING

The second step in formatting a hard drive involves creating partitions. Some operating systems include software you can use to create partitions. When you create a partition, you assign a drive letter to all or part of a hard drive. You must create at least one partition before you can use a new hard drive. You can also create additional partitions. Each partition acts as a separate hard drive and can have its own operating system. This allows you to store different types of data in each partition.

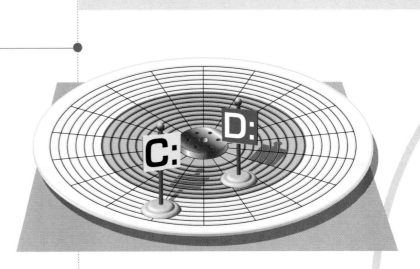

HIGH-LEVEL FORMAT

The last step in preparing a hard drive to store data is the high-level format. You can perform a high-level format using any operating system. During a high-level format, the operating system creates a table of contents for the hard drive. This prepares the hard drive to store and manage data. If the hard drive has multiple partitions, you will have to perform a high-level format on each partition individually.

Hard Drive (C:)
Table of Contents

TROUBLESHOOT AND REPAIR

Can I improve the performance of my hard drive?

If your hard drive operates slowly, you may be able to improve performance by defragmenting the drive. A fragmented hard drive stores parts of a file in many different locations. To retrieve a file, the computer must access many areas of the drive. You can use a defragmentation program to place all parts of a file in one location. This reduces the time the hard drive spends locating the file. Most operating systems have a defragmentation program you can use.

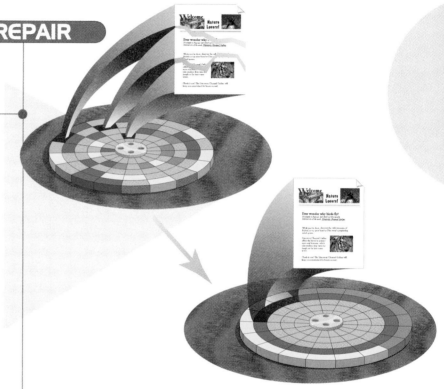

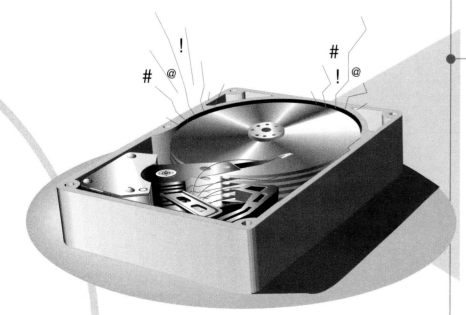

Why is my hard drive making noise?

The hard drive is one of the few mechanical devices in a computer. As with all mechanical devices, wear and tear can cause the moving parts to fail. Most hard drives make noise while they are operating, but unusual noises can be the first sign of a failing drive.

To prevent wear and tear and prolong the life of a hard drive, many new computers have hard drives that can be programmed to shut down after a specific period of inactivity.

Can I correct errors on my hard drive?

As the disks in a hard drive deteriorate, errors become more frequent when you try to access or store data on the drive. While the occasional error is normal, repeated errors may be an indication that the hard drive is about to fail.

You may be able to correct these errors by performing a high-level format to erase all the data on the drive. If the high-level format does not correct the problem, you can perform a low-level format. Check the documentation that came with the hard drive for more information about performing a low-level format.

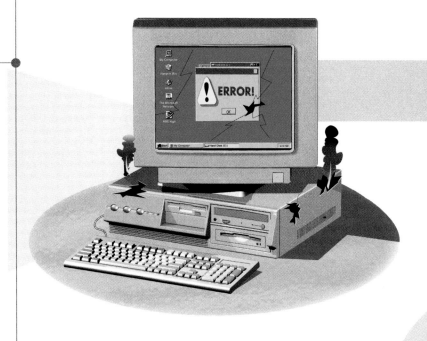

Can I recover data from a failed hard drive?

In most cases, you will not be able to recover data from a failed hard drive. When a hard drive fails, the read/write heads often touch, or crash into, the disks in the hard drive. This contact destroys the data on the disks.

FLOPPY DRIVE

REPLACE A FLOPPY DRIVE

A floppy drive stores and retrieves data on floppy disks. A floppy disk, also called a diskette, is a removable device that magnetically stores data.

Before replacing a floppy drive, turn off the computer, unplug the power cable and remove the cover from the computer case. Then ground yourself and the computer case. For information on grounding, see page 8.

Remove the screws that secure the floppy drive in the drive bay.

Disconnect the power supply cable from the back of the floppy drive.

Disconnect the ribbon cable from the back of the floppy drive. Then slide the drive out of the drive bay.

If necessary, attach a mounting bracket to the new floppy drive. Then slide the drive into the drive bay.

Connect the power supply cable and the ribbon cable to the back of the floppy drive.

Using small screws, secure the floppy drive in the drive bay. Then replace the cover on the computer case.

SET UP

How do I set up a floppy drive?

When you install a floppy drive, the computer may automatically detect and set up the drive for you. If the computer does not automatically detect and set up the floppy drive, you may need to change the computer's settings so it can work with the drive. For information on computer settings, see page 168.

Floppy drive detected

OK

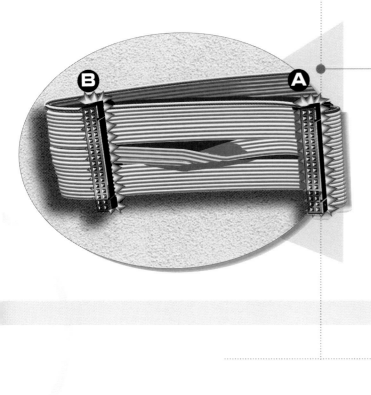

Can I install multiple floppy drives on my computer?

Many floppy drive ribbon cables have two connectors separated by a twist in the cable. This lets you install two floppy drives on a computer. If you install a single floppy drive on your computer, the drive is called drive A and must be attached to the connector after the twist in the cable. If you install another floppy drive, the second drive is called drive B and must be attached to the connector before the twist in the cable.

INSIDE A FLOPPY DRIVE

How does a floppy drive work?

Inside a floppy disk is a thin, plastic, flexible disk that magnetically stores data. The word floppy refers to this flexible disk. When you insert a floppy disk into a floppy drive, the flexible disk inside the floppy disk spins. The floppy drive has read/write heads that move across the flexible disk to read and record data on the disk.

CONSIDERATIONS

What type of floppy drive should I choose?

You should choose a floppy drive that can use disks with at least the same storage capacity as the floppy disks used by the people you want to exchange data with.

Most floppy drives use 3.5 inch floppy disks that can store up to 1.44 MB of data. Some newer types of floppy drives use 3.5 inch floppy disks that can store up to 200 MB of data.

A floppy drive designed for disks with a storage capacity of 1.44 MB cannot use disks with a higher capacity. However, floppy drives designed for higher capacity disks can also use disks with a capacity of 1.44 MB.

TROUBLESHOOT

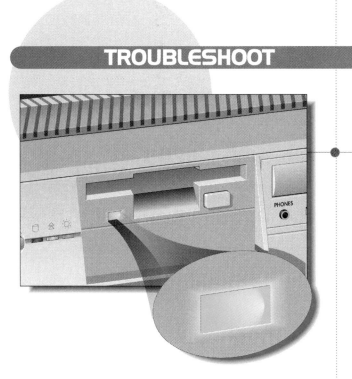

The floppy drive light is on continuously. What is wrong?

The floppy drive light is normally on when the floppy drive is accessing a floppy disk, but if the floppy drive light is on continuously, the drive may not be properly connected to the computer. You should make sure the ribbon cable is properly attached to the connector on the system board and to the connector on the back of the floppy drive.

Why do I get an error message when my floppy drive tries to access a floppy disk?

In most cases, if you get an error message, the disk is the cause of the problem. A floppy drive may not be able to access or store data on a defective disk.

To make sure errors are due to a floppy disk, try using another disk. If your floppy drive cannot access or store data on the second disk, you may need to clean the floppy drive. Cleaning kits that let you clean the inside of a floppy drive are available at most computer stores.

REMOVABLE STORAGE DEVICE

A removable storage device allows you to store large amounts of data on removable disks.

A removable disk is similar in size and shape to a floppy disk, but can store much more data.

INSTALL A REMOVABLE STORAGE DEVICE

Before installing a removable storage device, turn off the computer.

Connect the device cable to the port at the back of the removable storage device.

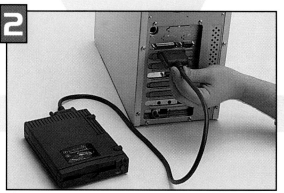

Connect the device cable to a parallel port at the back of the computer. Some removable storage devices connect to a SCSI port instead of a parallel port.

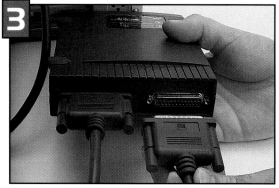

If you connected the device to a parallel port in step 2, you can connect the cable from your printer to the printer port on the back of the removable storage device.

Connect the power cable to the power connector on the removable storage device. Then plug the power cable into an electrical outlet.

INTERNAL REMOVABLE STORAGE DEVICE

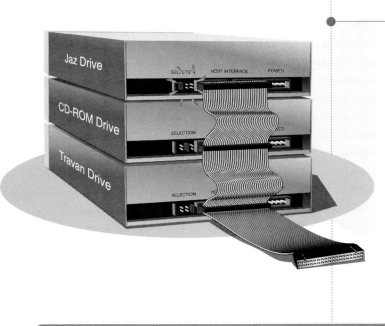

How do I install an internal removable storage device?

You can install an internal removable storage device the same way you install a CD-ROM drive. To install a CD-ROM drive, see page 146.

You may have to adjust the jumpers on an internal removable storage device so the device can work with the computer. Some internal removable storage devices use an Enhanced Integrated Drive Electronics (EIDE) ribbon cable to connect to a computer, while others use a Small Computer System Interface (SCSI) ribbon cable. If there are devices already attached to the ribbon cable, you may need to adjust the jumpers on the internal removable storage device. Consult the device's documentation for information on adjusting the jumpers.

SET UP

Do I need to install a driver for my removable storage device?

When you install a removable storage device, the computer may detect and set up the device, installing the necessary driver for you. If the computer does not install the driver, you may need to install the driver yourself.

CONSIDERATIONS

WHAT SHOULD I CONSIDER WHEN CHOOSING A REMOVABLE STORAGE DEVICE?

SPEED

Each removable storage device stores and accesses data at a specific speed. The type of device and how the device connects to the computer determine the speed.

MEDIA TYPE

Some removable disks contain a thin, flexible disk, similar to the media used in floppy disks. Other removable disks contain hard platters, similar to the media used in hard drives. Disks containing hard platters are usually faster and store more data than disks containing flexible media.

DISK CAPACITY

The amount of data a removable disk can store is measured in bytes. Some removable disks store up to 2 GB of data, while others store as little as 40 MB.

COST

Before purchasing a removable storage device, you should consider how much data you need to store and the cost per megabyte of storing the data. Inexpensive devices often use disks that cost more per megabyte than more expensive devices.

SOFTWARE

Removable storage devices usually include a variety of software that lets you use the device. For example, a removable storage device may come with software that allows you to back up data on your computer, copy the contents of disks or restore data after a computer crash.

MAINTAIN

How can I protect the data on my removable disks?

The data on a removable disk can be damaged if the disk is mishandled or exposed to magnetic fields. To avoid damage, store disks in a cool, dry, clean environment, away from the magnetic fields generated by your monitor and speakers.

How do I clean my removable storage device?

Most removable storage devices require only an occasional external cleaning with a damp cloth. Refer to the manufacturer's instructions for more information on cleaning the device.

TAPE DRIVE

A tape drive stores and retrieves data on tape cartridges. Most people use tape drives to make backup copies of files stored on a computer.

INSTALL A TAPE DRIVE

Before installing a tape drive, turn off the computer, unplug the power cable and remove the cover from the computer case. Then ground yourself and the computer case. For information on grounding, see page 8.

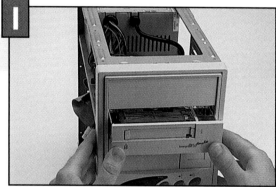

1 Using a slotted screwdriver, remove the drive bay cover from the drive bay on the front of the computer. Then slide the tape drive into the drive bay.

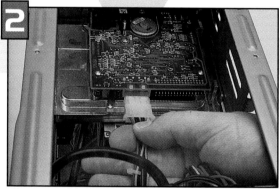

2 Connect a cable from the power supply to the tape drive.

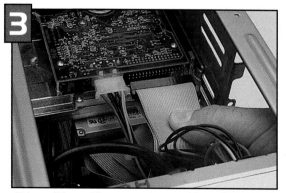

3 Using a ribbon cable, connect the tape drive to the computer.

4 Using small screws, secure the tape drive in the drive bay. Then replace the cover on the computer case.

SET UP

Do I need to adjust the jumpers on my tape drive?

Inexpensive tape drives use a floppy drive ribbon cable to connect to a computer, but many tape drives use a Small Computer System Interface (SCSI) ribbon cable. If there are devices already attached to the SCSI ribbon cable, you may need to adjust the jumpers on the tape drive. Consult the drive's documentation for information on adjusting the jumpers.

Do tape drives include installation software?

All tape drives include installation software you can use to install the necessary driver and set up the tape drive to work with your computer. You may also be able to use the installation software to optimize the performance of the drive.

EXTERNAL TAPE DRIVE

How do I install an external tape drive?

Position the external tape drive on your desk. Then connect the drive to a parallel or SCSI port at the back of your computer. You can then plug the power cable from the drive into an electrical outlet on the wall.

CONSIDERATIONS

WHAT SHOULD I CONSIDER WHEN CHOOSING A TAPE DRIVE?

COMPRESSION

Some tape drives can compress, or squeeze together, data so a tape cartridge can store more data. Depending on the type of data you are storing, compression can almost double the amount of data the tape cartridge can hold.

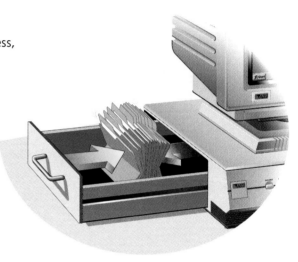

ACCESS TIME

The speed at which a tape drive retrieves data stored on a tape cartridge is called access time. The lower the access time, the faster the tape drive. A slow access time may be sufficient if you only occasionally restore data. If you regularly restore data, a fast access time is important.

BACKUP SOFTWARE

Most tape drives come with backup software that usually has limited features. You can purchase additional backup software that allows you to perform more advanced tasks, such as scheduling your backups.

TYPES OF TAPE DRIVES

WHAT TYPES OF TAPE DRIVES ARE AVAILABLE?

QIC DRIVE

A Quarter-Inch Cartridge (QIC, pronounced "quick") drive is commonly used with personal computers. A QIC drive is the slowest and least expensive type of drive. A high-quality QIC drive can store up to 10 GB of data.

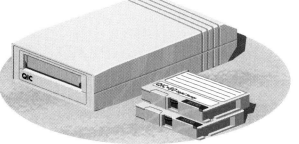

TRAVAN DRIVE

A Travan drive is a newer, faster type of QIC drive. A high-quality Travan drive can store up to 10 GB of data.

DAT DRIVE

A Digital Audio Tape (DAT) drive is a fast drive that is often used for backing up large amounts of data. A high-quality DAT drive can store up to 24 GB of data.

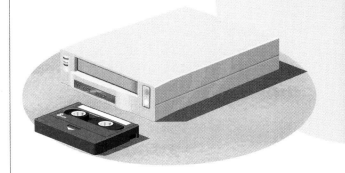

8 MM DRIVE

An 8 millimeter (mm) drive uses tape cartridges similar to the 8 mm tapes used in video cameras. A high-quality 8 mm drive can store up to 40 GB of data.

TAPE CARTRIDGES

How does a tape drive store and access data on a tape cartridge?

Inside a tape cartridge is a thin strip of plastic tape with a magnetic surface, similar to the tape found in audiotapes and videotapes. When you insert a tape cartridge into a tape drive, the tape moves across read/write heads in the tape drive. The read/write heads read and record data on the tape.

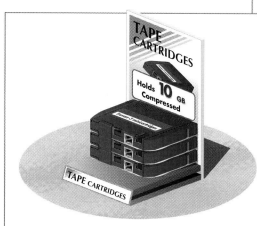

How much data can I store on a tape cartridge?

The amount of data you can store on a tape cartridge depends on the tape drive you use. When buying a tape drive, you should choose a drive that can store the entire contents of your hard drive on a single tape cartridge. This will make it easier to back up all the data on your hard drive.

Do tape cartridges require special care?

You should store tape cartridges in a dry location, away from direct sunlight. To prevent accidental erasure or damage, you should not store tape cartridges near devices that generate magnetic fields, such as speakers or monitors.

TROUBLESHOOT AND MAINTAIN

Should I test my tape drive and cartridges?

You should regularly restore data from tape cartridges to ensure that the tape drive is operating correctly and the tape cartridges are not damaged. Without regular testing, you could be performing backups on damaged cartridges without knowing there is a problem.

Why am I having problems restoring data from a tape cartridge?

The current backup software and the backup software used to store the data may be incompatible. To restore the data, you should use the same backup software that was used to back up the data originally.

How often should I clean my tape drive?

A tape drive may stop working if it is not cleaned regularly. Most tape drives need to be cleaned after a specific number of hours of use. Check the manufacturer's instructions for details on when to clean your tape drive.

You can use a cleaning cartridge to clean your tape drive. A cleaning cartridge is similar in size and shape to a tape cartridge.

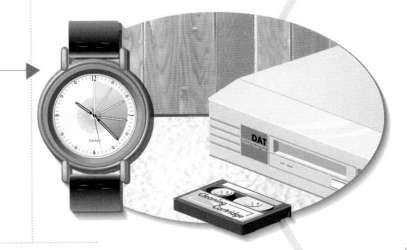

CD-ROM DRIVE

A CD-ROM drive is a device that reads information stored on CDs and CD-ROM discs.

INSTALL A CD-ROM DRIVE

Before installing a CD-ROM drive, turn off the computer, unplug the power cable and remove the cover from the computer case. Then ground yourself and the computer case. For information on grounding, see page 8.

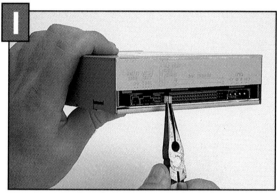

If necessary, adjust the jumpers on the back of the CD-ROM drive.

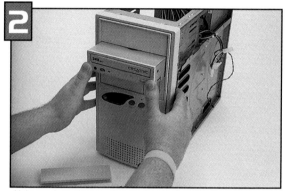

Using a slotted screwdriver, remove the drive bay cover from the drive bay on the front of the computer. Then slide the CD-ROM drive into the drive bay.

Connect a cable from the power supply to the CD-ROM drive.

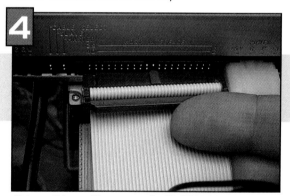

Using a ribbon cable, connect the CD-ROM drive to the computer.

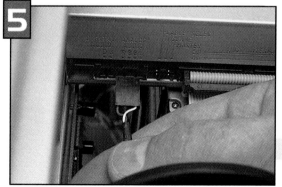

If necessary, connect the audio cable to the CD-ROM drive. Then connect the audio cable to the sound card. This allows your computer's speakers to play sound from compact discs.

Using small screws, secure the CD-ROM drive in the drive bay. Then replace the cover on the computer case.

SET UP

Will my computer automatically detect the CD-ROM drive?

Your computer may automatically detect and set up a CD-ROM drive you install. If your computer does not set up the drive, you may need to change the computer's settings. For information on computer settings, see page 168.

Do I need to adjust the jumpers on my CD-ROM drive?

If you use an EIDE ribbon cable to connect the CD-ROM drive and another device to the computer, you may have to change the jumpers on the devices. One device must be set as the master, while the other is set as the slave.

You may also need to adjust the jumpers on the CD-ROM drive if you are using a SCSI ribbon cable to connect multiple devices. Each device must be assigned a unique number from zero to seven.

Consult the drive's documentation for information on adjusting the jumpers.

Do I need to install a driver?

You may need to install a driver before you can use the CD-ROM drive. Consult the drive's documentation for information on installing a driver.

CONSIDERATIONS

WHAT SHOULD I CONSIDER WHEN CHOOSING A CD-ROM DRIVE?

SPEED

The speed of a CD-ROM drive is indicated by a number followed by an X and determines how fast a disc spins. The faster a disc spins, the faster information transfers from the disc to the computer, which results in better performance. Most new CD-ROM drives have a speed of at least 20X.

CD-RECORDABLE DRIVE

A CD-Recordable (CD-R) drive allows you to store your own information on a disc. This type of drive is useful for backing up a hard drive or distributing information. A CD-Recordable drive can record information on each disc only once. A CD-Recordable disc can store up to 650 MB of data.

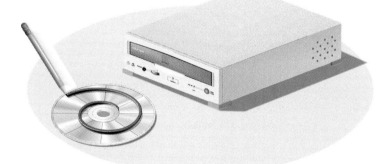

CD-REWRITABLE DRIVE

A CD-ReWritable (CD-RW) drive is similar to a CD-Recordable drive, but allows you to change the data you record on a disc many times. A CD-Rewritable disc stores the same amount of data as a CD-Recordable disc.

TROUBLESHOOT AND MAINTAIN

Why can't my CD-ROM drive access information on a disc?

If your CD-ROM drive cannot access information on a disc, the disc may not be compatible with the drive. Some discs, such as discs created using a CD-Recordable or CD-Rewritable drive, are not compatible with all CD-ROM drives.

My CD-ROM drive sounds like it is constantly running. Is something wrong?

If your CD-ROM drive sounds like it is constantly running, the disc in the drive may be scratched and the drive may not be able to access the information on the disc. To prevent scratches, you should handle only the outer edge of your discs.

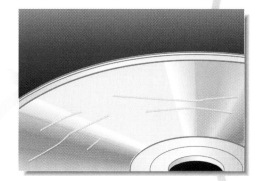

How do I clean my CD-ROM drive?

Over time, dust and dirt can accumulate inside a CD-ROM drive. This may prevent the CD-ROM drive from reading information on a disc. You should use a cleaning kit to clean the inside of your CD-ROM drive on a regular basis. CD-ROM drive cleaning kits are available at most computer stores.

DVD-ROM DRIVE

A DVD-ROM drive is a device that reads information stored on DVD-ROM discs.

A DVD-ROM disc can store up to 4.7 GB of information, including programs and multimedia.

Before installing a DVD-ROM drive, turn off the computer, unplug the power cable and remove the cover from the computer case. Then ground yourself and the computer case. For information on grounding, see page 8.

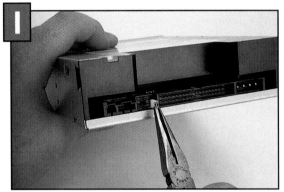

If necessary, adjust the jumpers on the back of the DVD-ROM drive.

Using a slotted screwdriver, remove the drive bay cover from the drive bay on the front of the computer. Then slide the DVD-ROM drive into the drive bay.

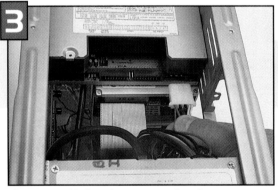

Connect a cable from the power supply to the DVD-ROM drive.

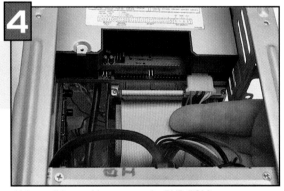

Using a ribbon cable, connect the DVD-ROM drive to the computer.

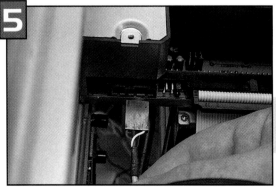

If necessary, connect the audio cable to the DVD-ROM drive. Then connect the audio cable to the sound card. This allows your computer's speakers to play sound from DVD-ROM discs.

Using small screws, secure the DVD-ROM drive in the drive bay. Then replace the cover on the computer case.

SET UP

Do I need to adjust the jumpers on my DVD-ROM drive?

Most DVD-ROM drives use an Enhanced Integrated Drive Electronics (EIDE) ribbon cable to connect to a computer, but some DVD-ROM drives use a Small Computer System Interface (SCSI) ribbon cable. If there are devices already attached to the EIDE or SCSI ribbon cable, you may need to adjust the jumpers on the DVD-ROM drive. Consult the drive's documentation for information on adjusting the jumpers.

Does my DVD-ROM drive come with an installation program?

Every DVD-ROM drive comes with an installation program that contains the software the DVD-ROM drive needs to operate.

CONSIDERATIONS

Can DVD-ROM drives read all types of discs?

All DVD-ROM drives can read DVD-ROM discs, CD-ROM discs and music CDs. Some early DVD-ROM drives, called first generation drives, cannot read discs recorded on a CD-Recordable (CD-R) or CD-ReWritable (CD-RW) drive. When choosing a DVD-ROM drive, make sure you select a second generation drive that can read CD-R and CD-RW discs.

CHAPTER 6

MAINTAIN A COMPUTER

Regular maintenance can help ensure the smooth operation of your computer. In this chapter, learn how to clean your computer, avoid destructive viruses and back up important information.

CLEAN A COMPUTER

WHAT ITEMS CAN I USE TO CLEAN MY COMPUTER?

There are many items you can use to clean a computer. Cleaning your computer on a regular basis can help keep the computer in good working order.

CLEANING FLUID

You can use cleaning fluid to clean the plastic surfaces on the outside of a computer. Computer cleaning fluid usually comes in a spray bottle and is available at most computer stores.

You should always spray cleaning fluid on a cloth rather than directly on a computer. This will prevent the fluid from leaking inside the computer and causing electrical problems.

BRUSH

You can use a small brush, such as a makeup brush or paintbrush, to remove dirt and debris from inside a computer. You may also want to use a brush to loosen accumulated dust before removing the dust with a can of compressed air or a computer vacuum cleaner. You should not use a brush on the circuit boards inside a computer.

COMPRESSED AIR

You can use a can of compressed air to blow dirt, debris and dust from inside a computer. Cans of compressed air are inexpensive and are available at most computer stores.

VACUUM CLEANER

You can remove dust and dirt from inside a computer using a specially designed vacuum cleaner. A computer vacuum cleaner is useful when you want to avoid blowing dust on other components. These vacuum cleaners often come with attachments you can use to clean very small areas of a computer, such as between the keys on a keyboard or between expansion slots. Computer vacuum cleaners are available at most computer stores.

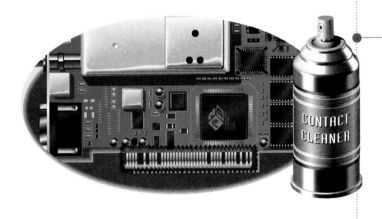

CONTACT CLEANER

You can use contact cleaner to clean the connectors in a computer, such as expansion slot connectors and the metal contacts on memory modules. Cleaning connectors helps ensure a reliable connection between a component and the computer. Contact cleaner is available at most computer stores.

VIRUS PROTECTION
AND DETECTION

HOW CAN I PROTECT MY COMPUTER FROM VIRUSES?

There are several ways you can protect your computer from viruses.

A virus is a program that can disrupt the normal operation of a computer. The symptoms of a virus are often mistaken for hardware or software problems. Common symptoms of a virus can include computer lockups, data loss, reduced hard drive space, program crashes, unusual messages and reduced computer performance.

HOW VIRUSES SPREAD

FLOPPY DISK

Floppy disks are a common way that viruses spread between computers. You should not use a floppy disk you receive from another person unless you are certain the disk does not contain a virus. You should also never start a computer when the floppy drive contains a disk that has been used by another computer.

INTERNET

The Internet has made it possible for viruses to spread quickly to many computers. You should only download programs or other information from reputable sources on the Internet.

You should also be careful of files you receive attached to e-mail messages. You should only open files sent by people you trust.

ANTI-VIRUS PROGRAMS

To maximize virus protection, you should use more than one type of anti-virus program. Two of the most popular types of anti-virus programs are scanners and memory-resident scanners.

SCANNER

You can run a virus scanner to check the files on a hard drive or floppy disk for viruses. You can run this type of anti-virus program as a preventative measure or when symptoms of a virus are present. Most scanners also include a virus-removal program.

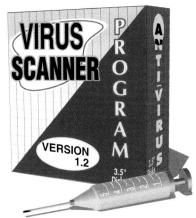

MEMORY-RESIDENT SCANNER

A memory-resident virus scanner constantly runs in the background of a computer and automatically checks for viruses. Memory-resident scanners offer better protection than regular scanners, since memory-resident scanners can detect a virus before the virus can do serious damage. Most memory-resident scanners also include a virus-removal program.

ANTI-VIRUS PROGRAM UPDATES

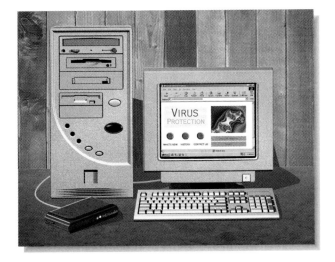

Hundreds of new viruses are developed each year. Anti-virus program manufacturers regularly release updates that allow their programs to detect the latest known viruses. You should check the manufacturer's Web site to ensure the anti-virus programs you use are up-to-date.

BACK UP INFORMATION

HOW CAN I PROTECT THE INFORMATION STORED ON MY COMPUTER DURING AN UPGRADE OR REPAIR?

Before you upgrade or repair your computer, you should ensure you have a backup copy of all the information stored on the computer.

You are more likely to lose or damage information on a hard drive while upgrading or repairing a computer than at any other time.

BACKUP SCHEDULE

You should create and then strictly follow a backup schedule. To determine how often you should back up the information on a computer, consider the importance of the information and the time it would take to recreate your work. In the event of a hard drive failure, you will lose all the work you have accomplished since the last backup you performed.

BACKUP MEDIA MAINTENANCE

You can back up information onto media such as floppy disks, tape cartridges or removable disks. You should store your backup media in a safe, dry location out of direct sunlight.

BACKUP PROCEDURES

The backup procedures you can perform depend on the capabilities of your backup software.

FULL BACKUP

A full backup can back up all the programs and information on a computer. You may want to perform a full backup before you upgrade or repair a computer.

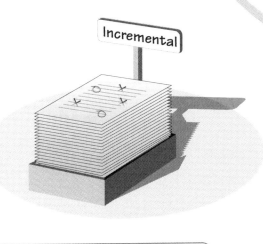

Full

DIFFERENTIAL BACKUP

A differential backup backs up only the information that has changed since the last full backup. To restore a differential backup, you must restore the last full backup and the last differential backup that was performed.

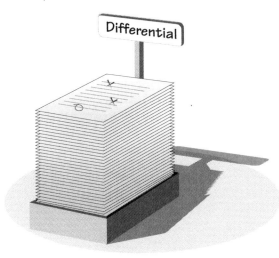

Differential

Incremental

INCREMENTAL BACKUP

An incremental backup backs up only the information that has changed since the last time you performed any type of backup. To restore an incremental backup, you must restore the last full backup and all the backups made since the last full backup.

CHAPTER 7

UPGRADE A COMPUTER

You can upgrade your computer to increase the computer's capabilities. This chapter will explain how to upgrade your software and operating system and much more.

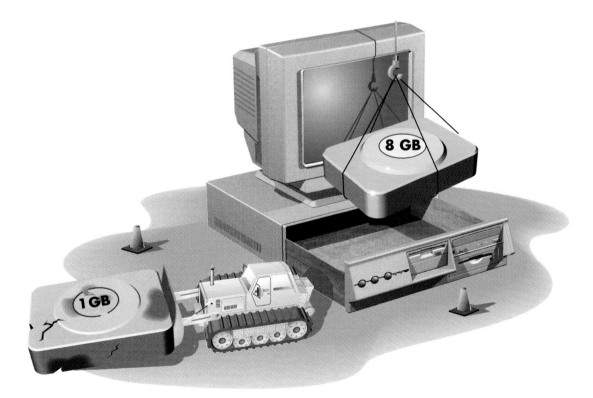

UPGRADE A COMPUTER

WHAT FACTORS SHOULD I CONSIDER BEFORE UPGRADING MY COMPUTER?

After deciding to upgrade, you should consider the various ways to upgrade your computer.

You can upgrade a computer by adding a new component or replacing a current component with one that offers more features.

DETERMINE IF YOU NEED TO UPGRADE

CONSIDER CURRENT NEEDS

You should consider how you currently use the computer and then determine if the computer could better meet your needs. For example, if you mainly use a computer for word processing, you may want to upgrade the keyboard to a style that allows you to work more comfortably or includes built-in enhancements, such as a trackball.

CONSIDER FUTURE NEEDS

You should consider how you want to use the computer in the future. You may want to upgrade a computer that is not capable of adequately meeting your future needs. For example, if you intend to use a computer to play games, you may want to upgrade to a fast CD-ROM drive or install a high-quality sound card.

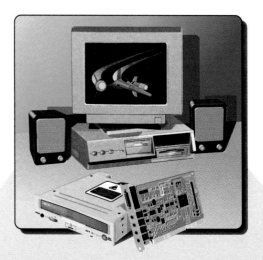

WAYS TO UPGRADE

INCREASE CAPABILITIES

You can upgrade a computer by increasing the computer's capabilities. This lets you use the computer to perform new tasks. For example, adding a TV tuner card to a computer lets you use the computer to watch television programs.

IMPROVE EFFICIENCY

You can improve the efficiency of a computer by upgrading a component to a faster model. Modems, CPUs and CD-ROM drives are examples of components you can replace with faster models to upgrade a computer.

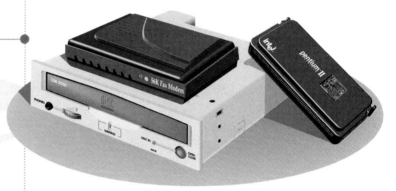

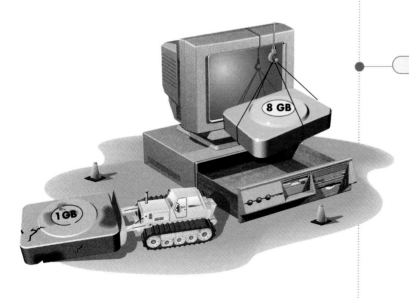

REPLACE FAILING COMPONENTS

Many people upgrade their computers by replacing a failing component. For example, when a hard drive fails, you may want to consider upgrading to a hard drive with more storage capacity.

You may have no choice but to upgrade a failing component if the original model is no longer available. For example, hard drives with capacities of less than 2 GB are no longer manufactured.

RESOURCE SETTINGS

WHAT ARE RESOURCE SETTINGS?

Resource settings allow the devices installed on a computer to communicate with the computer.

Each device has its own unique resource settings. You can check the documentation included with a device to determine which resource settings it can use.

RESOURCE CONFLICT

If two devices installed on a computer require the same resource settings, the devices may not work properly. This is known as a resource conflict. Resource conflicts are the most common cause of problems when installing a device. To resolve a conflict, you must change the resource settings for one of the devices.

RECORD RESOURCE SETTINGS

You should record the resource settings used by each device on your computer. If you change the resource settings for a device, you should note the change. By keeping an accurate record of the resource settings used by devices, you will be better able to resolve any resource conflicts you encounter when installing a new device on your computer.

ADJUST RESOURCE SETTINGS

Jumpers

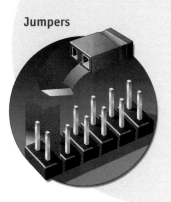

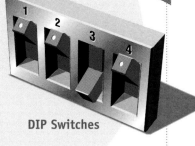

DIP Switches

HARDWARE

You can physically adjust the resource settings on some devices. If a device uses jumpers, you can adjust the resource settings by placing a small plastic plug over pins on the device. Other devices require you to adjust the resource settings using a series of small switches, called DIP switches.

SOFTWARE

Many devices come with software you can use to adjust the resource settings for the device. The software saves the resource settings on a memory chip located on the device. The memory chip can store the resource settings even when the computer is turned off.

New video card found!
Adjusting resource settings...

OK   Cancel

PLUG AND PLAY

Most new computers use Plug and Play technology. When you install a Plug and Play device, the computer will detect the device and automatically adjust the resource settings for the device.

RESOURCE SETTINGS

IRQ

A device uses an Interrupt Request (IRQ) to alert the CPU that the device needs attention. Each device installed on a computer has its own IRQ setting. You cannot change the IRQ setting for some devices.

Common IRQ Settings

0	Computer timer	7	Parallel port
1	Keyboard	8	Clock
3	Serial port 2	12	Mouse port
4	Serial port 1	14	Primary hard drive
5	Sound card	15	Secondary hard drive
6	Floppy drive		

DMA CHANNEL

Common DMA channel Settings

1	Sound card	5	Sound card or SCSI card
2	Floppy drive	6	Sound card or network interface card
3	Parallel port or voice modem		

Each device in a computer that exchanges data with the computer's memory requires the use of the CPU. A Direct Memory Access (DMA) channel allows a device to bypass the CPU and exchange data directly with the computer's memory. This speeds up the processing of information and improves the performance of the computer.

I/O ADDRESS

An Input/Output (I/O) address allows a device to communicate with the computer's CPU. Most devices in a computer have their own I/O address. The CPU uses a device's I/O address to exchange data with the device. I/O addresses are also called base addresses.

Common I/O Address Settings

220	Sound card	370	Parallel port
2F0	Serial port 2	3F0	Serial port 1
300	Network interface card		

MEMORY ADDRESS

Common Memory Address Settings

C0000	Video card	D0000	Network interface card
C8000	Hard drive	F0000	BIOS

Some devices, such as hard drives, transmit a lot of data and require a portion of the computer's memory to temporarily store the data being transferred. A memory address specifies the portion of a computer's memory where a device can temporarily store data.

COMPUTER SETTINGS

HOW CAN I CHANGE MY COMPUTER'S SETTINGS?

You can use the BIOS to change your computer's settings.

BIOS

The Basic Input/Output System (BIOS) is a chip on your system board that allows you to access and change your computer's settings. When you install a new device on your computer, the BIOS will usually change your computer's settings so the computer can work with the new device. If the BIOS does not automatically change your computer's settings, you can use the BIOS setup program to change the computer's settings yourself.

CMOS

Your computer's settings are stored in another chip on the system board, called the Complementary Metal Oxide Semiconductor (CMOS) chip. Any changes you make to your computer's settings using the BIOS setup program are saved in the CMOS. A small battery allows the CMOS to save your computer's settings even when the computer is turned off.

BIOS SETUP PROGRAM

DOCUMENTATION

The BIOS setup program is different for many computers. You should always consult the documentation that came with your computer or system board before accessing or changing any settings in the BIOS.

ACCESS

Most computers let you access the BIOS setup program by pressing a specific key as the computer starts. Some computers also let you use configuration software to access the BIOS setup program after the computer has started.

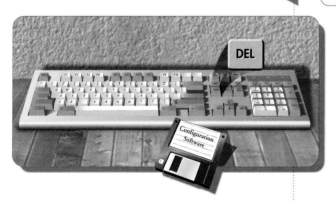

INTERFACE

Most BIOS setup programs have a text-based interface, which allows you to select and change computer settings from a menu using the keys on your keyboard. Some BIOS setup programs have a Graphical User Interface (GUI, pronounced "gooey"), which allows you to use a pointing device to select pictures to change your computer's settings.

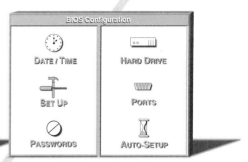

Text-based Interface   Graphical User Interface

COMMON COMPUTER SETTINGS

BOOT SEQUENCE

The boot sequence contains information about the order that your computer checks storage devices for an operating system when you turn on the computer. Most computers begin with the floppy drive and then check the hard drive. You can change the boot sequence to change the order that your computer checks storage devices.

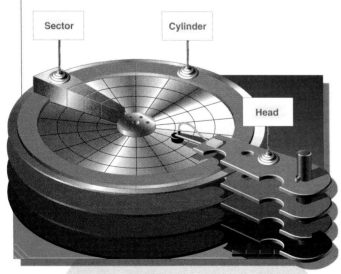

HARD DRIVE

You can specify the settings for your hard drive, including the number of cylinders, heads and sectors the hard drive uses. A hard drive's settings are usually printed on the drive or in the documentation included with the drive.

POWER MANAGEMENT

You can change the power management settings on your computer. Power management allows you to conserve energy by controlling how the computer uses power after a period of inactivity. For example, you can have your computer enter a low power, or standby, mode after ten minutes of inactivity.

STORAGE DEVICE

You can adjust the settings for the storage devices, such as a floppy or CD-ROM drive, installed on your computer. For example, you can specify the storage capacity of a floppy drive installed on your computer.

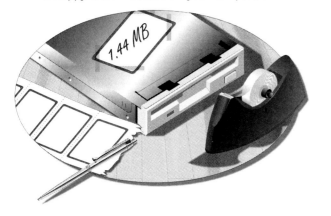

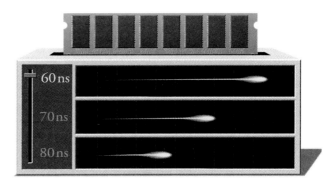

MEMORY SPEED

The memory in most computers can operate at different speeds. Many BIOS setup programs allow you to adjust the speed of the memory.

PASSWORD

You can assign a password to prevent people from accessing the BIOS setup program and changing your computer's settings. Many BIOS setup programs also allow you to assign a password to prevent other people from using your computer.

CONNECTOR

You can adjust the settings for connectors, such as USB or parallel ports, on your computer. You can also enable or disable connectors on your computer.

UPGRADE AN
OPERATING SYSTEM

WHY WOULD I UPGRADE MY OPERATING SYSTEM?

An operating system determines the hardware and software you can install on your computer. You can upgrade your operating system so you can use hardware or software that your current operating system does not support.

An operating system is the software that controls the overall activity of a computer. An operating system ensures that all parts of a computer system work together smoothly and efficiently.

MS-DOS

WINDOWS

OPERATING SYSTEM FUNCTIONS

CONTROL HARDWARE

An operating system controls the different parts of a computer system and enables all the parts to work together.

RUN APPLICATION SOFTWARE

An operating system runs application software, such as Microsoft Word and Lotus 1-2-3.

MANAGE INFORMATION

An operating system provides ways to manage and organize information stored on a computer. You can use an operating system to sort, copy, move, delete and view files.

UPGRADE CONSIDERATIONS

EASE OF USE

Before upgrading, you should try using a computer running the operating system you want to upgrade to. This allows you to make sure the operating system is easy to use.

MINIMUM REQUIREMENTS

You must ensure that your computer meets the minimum requirements the operating system needs to work properly. For example, most operating systems require a computer to have a certain amount of memory and hard drive space.

System Requirements
- 486/66 MHz CPU or higher
- 16 MB RAM
- Minimum install: 120 MB
- Display: VGA or better
- Mouse or other pointing device

TROUBLESHOOT AN UPGRADE

HARDWARE SETTINGS

If a hardware device no longer works after you upgrade your operating system, you may need to change the settings for the operating system. Consult the documentation that came with the operating system for information on how to change the settings. You may also need to change your computer's settings. For information on computer settings, see page 168.

SOFTWARE COMPATIBILITY

If your application software is not working properly, the application may be incompatible with the new operating system. You may need to upgrade the software to work with the new operating system.

TYPES OF OPERATING SYSTEMS

MS-DOS

MS-DOS stands for Microsoft Disk Operating System. This operating system displays lines of text on the screen and allows you to perform tasks by entering text commands. MS-DOS was the most popular operating system when personal computers were first available.

```
C:\> DIR\DATA\123DATA

Volume in drive C has no label
Volume Serial Number is 12FA-3823
Directory of C:\DATA\123DATA

                  <DIR>           03-10-95   2:43p
                  <DIR>           01-10-95   3:15p
INCOME1Q WK4          10,005 04-08-95   9:01a
INCOME2Q WK4          15,609 02-16-95   9:23a
INCOME3Q WK4          12,444 03-10-95   4:20p
JIM      WK4          11,959 03-15-95   9:55a
PLAN1    WK4          13,999 01-08-95   1:40p
PLAN2    WK4          17,909 02-15-95   9:43a
PLAN3    WK4          11,555 04-20-95   8:54p
PROJECT1 WK4          12,202 01-17-95   2:04p
PROJECT2 WK4          15,898 02-15-95   2:20p
PROJECT3 WK4          19,345 02-08-95   9:09a
          12 file(s)         140,925 bytes
                         96,026,624 bytes free

C:\>
```

WINDOWS 95

Windows 95 is the successor of Windows 3.1. Windows 95 is more graphical than Windows 3.1 and is a true operating system because it does not need MS-DOS to operate. Windows 95 includes many advanced features such as support for Plug and Play technology, performance-enhancing programs and the ability to share information and printers on a network.

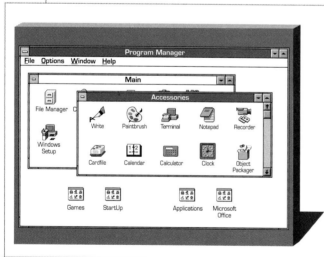

WINDOWS 3.1

Windows 3.1 was the first widely used Graphical User Interface (GUI, pronounced "gooey"). A GUI allows you to use graphics instead of text commands to perform tasks. Windows 3.1 is not a true operating system because it needs MS-DOS to operate.

WINDOWS 98

Windows 98 is the successor of Windows 95. This operating system is similar to Windows 95 but includes many improved features. For example, Windows 98 includes tools you can use to find and fix computer problems and a file system that better manages data on large hard drives to reduce wasted space. Windows 98 also includes Internet-related programs, including a Web browser and e-mail program.

WINDOWS NT

Windows NT is the most powerful version of the Windows operating system and provides excellent security features. Windows NT is easy to use and has the same look and feel as Windows 95 and Windows 98.

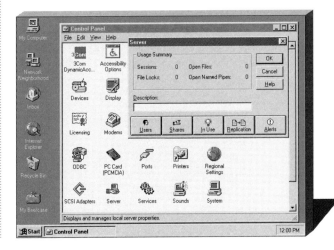

UNIX

UNIX is a powerful operating system you can use to run a single computer or an entire network. UNIX is harder to install and set up than most operating systems, but has many built-in security features and provides greater control over a computer's resources and power.

UPGRADE SOFTWARE

ARE THERE ANY ISSUES I SHOULD CONSIDER BEFORE UPGRADING THE SOFTWARE ON MY COMPUTER?

There are several issues you should consider before upgrading software.

Upgrading software can improve the way you accomplish specific tasks on your computer.

Before

After

TYPES OF UPGRADES

NEW VERSION

All software has a version number. When a manufacturer adds new features to existing software, the upgraded software is given a higher number than the previous version. This helps people identify the most up-to-date software. For example, Internet Explorer 4.0 is a more recent version of the Web browser than Internet Explorer 3.0.

PATCH

Manufacturers create minor software upgrades, called patches, to make corrections or improvements to software. You can often find a patch on the software manufacturer's Web site. You can also contact the manufacturer to obtain a patch on a floppy disk.

UPGRADE CONSIDERATIONS

NEW CAPABILITIES

Most software is upgraded at least once every year or two to add new capabilities or improved features to the software. In some cases, the new capabilities increase the complexity of the software, causing the software to operate slower than the previous version. You should upgrade software only when you need new capabilities.

COST

Software upgrades vary in price, but are usually less expensive than hardware upgrades. Upgrading software can be an effective way to increase the capabilities and performance of your computer without spending a lot of money. For example, instead of purchasing a new modem, you can download a faster Web browser from the World Wide Web for free.

Minimum Requirements
- Pentium 133 MHz or higher
- Windows 95 or higher
- Memory: 32 MB
- Minimum install: 100 MB
- Monitor: SVGA or above
- Mouse or other pointing device

COMPATIBILITY

If you decide to upgrade your software, make sure you choose software that is compatible with your operating system. You should also check the minimum requirements for the software upgrade. A new software version often requires more memory and hard drive space than the previous version.

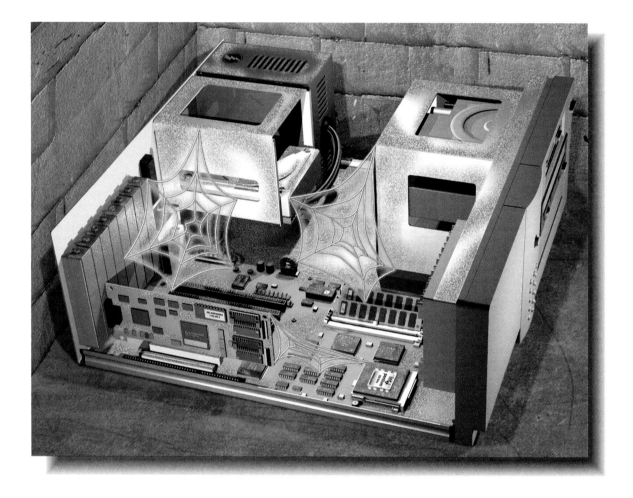

CHAPTER 8

REPAIR A COMPUTER

Locating the cause of a computer malfunction is the first step towards repairing it. This chapter shows you how to troubleshoot hardware and software problems, when to consult a repair service and much more.

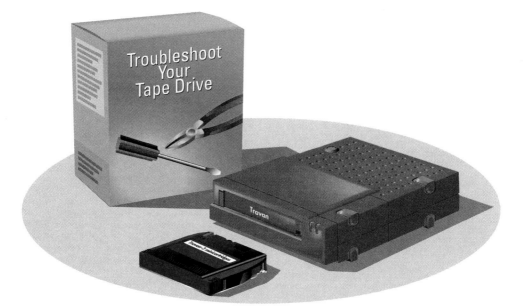

HARDWARE FAILURE

WHAT ARE THE MOST COMMON CAUSES OF HARDWARE FAILURE?

There are several common causes of hardware failure. Being aware of the causes of hardware failure can help you avoid problems.

A loose connection between a computer and a component can give the appearance of a hardware failure. You should always make sure components are securely connected to the computer.

COMPONENT AGE

Many components simply fail after they have been used for several years. Components, such as hard drives, floppy drives and fans, that contain moving parts eventually wear out. If properly maintained, most computer components can last 5 years or more.

DEFECTIVE COMPONENTS

Defects can cause a component to fail when it is first installed in a computer or after only a week or month of use. Although the quality and reliability of new components has increased in recent years, up to 20 percent of new components are defective when they are purchased.

POWER FLUCTUATIONS

One of the most common causes of hardware failure is repeated exposure to power fluctuations, such as spikes, surges and blackouts. You can connect a computer to an Uninterruptible Power Supply (UPS) to protect the computer from power fluctuations. For information on uninterruptible power supplies, see page 104.

HEAT

All computer components generate heat as they operate. If the temperature in a computer gets too high, hardware failures can occur. To prevent overheating, you should always ensure that a computer has adequate ventilation and that the fan at the back of the computer is not blocked.

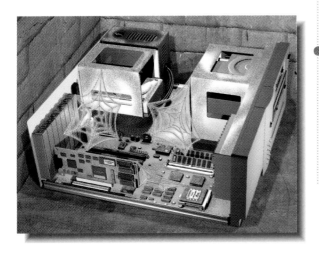

DUST AND DIRT

Dust and dirt inside a computer are a common cause of hardware failure. Dust and dirt can cause increased temperatures and short-circuiting inside a computer. You should clean a computer on a regular basis to keep hardware in good working order. For information on cleaning a computer, see page 154.

TROUBLESHOOT A HARDWARE PROBLEM

HOW CAN I FIND THE CAUSE OF A HARDWARE PROBLEM?

Troubleshooting can help you find the cause of a hardware problem and may help you fix the problem.

When troubleshooting a hardware problem, you should focus on one component at a time, beginning with the component you think is causing the problem.

CHECK CONNECTIONS

A loose connection is a common cause of hardware problems. Make sure the component is securely connected to the computer.

TEST MULTIPLE POSSIBILITIES

Testing multiple possibilities can help you find the cause of a problem. For example, if a floppy drive cannot access data on a floppy disk, the problem may be caused by the drive or the disk. To find the cause, try using another disk. If the floppy drive cannot access data on the second disk, the drive is likely the cause of the problem.

CHECK THE DRIVER

Most computer components require software, called a driver, to operate. You should ensure you are using the correct and most up-to-date driver for the component you think is causing the problem.

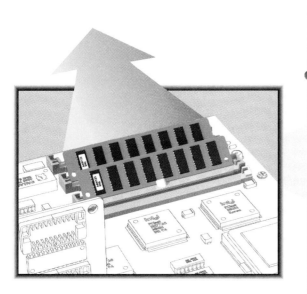

ELIMINATE THE POSSIBILITIES

You may be able to determine the cause of a problem by removing components from a computer one at a time and restarting the computer to see if the problem still exists. For example, if a computer displays a memory error, you can try removing one bank of memory modules at a time. If the memory error stops, the last bank of memory modules you removed may be the cause of the problem.

TRY ANOTHER COMPONENT

You can try using another component to troubleshoot a problem. For example, if you think the video card is malfunctioning, try replacing it with a video card you know works properly. If the problem stops, the original video card is likely the cause of the problem.

MOVE A COMPONENT

Moving a component can help you troubleshoot a problem. For example, if you suspect an expansion card is causing a problem, you can move the card to another expansion slot. If the problem persists, it is likely due to the expansion card. If the problem stops, it may be due to the original expansion slot.

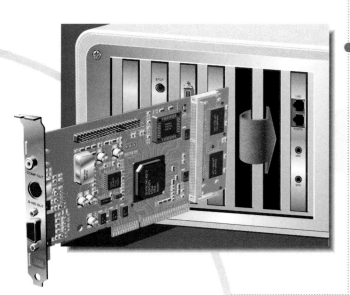

TROUBLESHOOT A SOFTWARE PROBLEM

HOW CAN I TROUBLESHOOT A SOFTWARE PROBLEM?

There are several things you can do to find the cause of a software problem. Troubleshooting may also help you fix the problem.

Software problems such as program crashes, error messages and system lockups are often caused by corrupt program files. When troubleshooting a software problem, you should start with the program you most recently installed on the computer. A corrupt program may begin causing problems shortly after it is installed.

To avoid accidentally corrupting or deleting files your programs need to operate, you should always exit all open programs and properly shut down the operating system before turning off a computer.

CHECK FOR VIRUSES

Software problems may be caused by a computer virus. You can use an anti-virus program to check the computer for viruses. Most anti-virus programs also include a virus-removal program you can use if you find a virus. For information on viruses and anti-virus programs, see page 156.

RE-INSTALL SOFTWARE

If a problem only occurs when you use a specific program, you may be able to correct the problem by re-installing the software. Re-installing software replaces the program files on the computer with a new copy. If the cause of a problem is deleted or corrupted program files, re-installing the software may correct the problem.

UNINSTALL SOFTWARE

If you suspect the problems you are experiencing are caused by a particular program, you can remove the program to see if the problems stop. Most programs come with a utility that lets you uninstall the program. Some operating systems, such as Windows 95 and Windows 98, also include an uninstall utility you can use to help remove a program.

RE-INSTALL OPERATING SYSTEM

If you are experiencing problems with all the programs installed on a computer, the operating system may be the cause of the problems. An operating system can become corrupted when system files are accidentally deleted or damaged. Re-installing the operating system may resolve the problems.

A diagnostic program may help you locate and repair computer problems.

IS THERE A PROGRAM THAT CAN HELP ME LOCATE AND REPAIR PROBLEMS WITH MY COMPUTER?

All personal computers have a basic, built-in diagnostic program, called the Power-On Self Test (POST). For information on the POST, see page 188.

WHERE TO FIND DIAGNOSTIC PROGRAMS

Most operating systems, such as Windows 95 and Windows 98, include some diagnostic programs. You can also buy many commercial diagnostic programs at computer stores. Popular commercial diagnostic programs include CyberMedia's First Aid and Symantec's Norton Utilities.

TROUBLESHOOT USING DIAGNOSTIC PROGRAMS

You can set up most diagnostic programs to run diagnostic tests repeatedly and report any errors that are detected. This is useful if you are trying to troubleshoot a problem that occurs from time to time and you need to run the diagnostic program for an extended period, such as overnight.

TYPES OF DIAGNOSTIC PROGRAMS

HARD DRIVE

A hard drive diagnostic program can help you locate and repair errors on a hard drive. Most hard drive diagnostic programs can also help improve the performance of a hard drive.

MEMORY

A memory diagnostic program allows you to check for errors in a computer's memory. Memory diagnostic programs are also useful for displaying the amount of memory in a computer and the amount of memory required by individual programs.

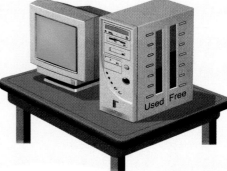

SOFTWARE

Operating systems and other software can cause many computer problems. A software diagnostic program inspects all the software installed on a computer to ensure the software is operating correctly.

SPECIALIZED PROGRAMS

Many computer components and devices come with their own specialized diagnostic programs. Items such as video cards, network interface cards and removable storage devices often come with diagnostic programs that you can use to test the item for errors.

ERROR CODES

Each time you turn on your computer, the computer performs a series of tests, called the Power-On Self Test (POST). The POST determines whether the main components in the computer, such as the system board and hard drive, are functioning properly. If a component is malfunctioning, the computer generates an error code.

ERROR CODES

If the computer detects an error during the POST and the video card and monitor are working properly, the computer will display an error code on the screen.

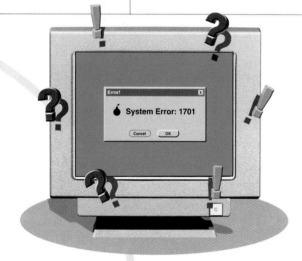

The error codes your computer displays depend on the type of system board in the computer. For example, some computers display only an error number, while other computers may display an error number and a short message explaining the error. You should always consult the documentation that came with your computer or system board to determine the exact cause of an error and how to repair the error.

Common Error Codes	
Error Number	Problem
101 - 199	System board error
201 - 299	RAM error
301 - 399	Keyboard error
601 - 699	Floppy drive error
901 - 999	Printer port error
1101 - 1199	Serial port error
1701 - 1799	Hard drive error

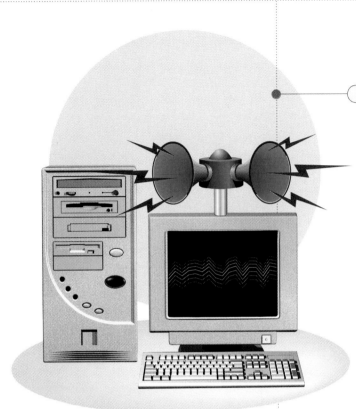

BEEP ERROR CODES

If the computer finds an error during the POST and the video card is not working properly, the computer will generate a beep error code. Beep error codes usually mean that the computer will not be able to start until the error is fixed.

The beep error codes your computer generates depend on the type of system board in the computer. For example, some computers may generate a series of short and long beeps, while other computers generate only short beeps. You should always consult the documentation that came with your computer or system board to determine what a beep error code means before attempting to repair the error.

COMMON BEEP ERROR CODES

Note: All computers normally generate a single beep when they start up. If a computer beeps once and continues to start up, there is no error.

Common Beep Error Codes	
No. of Beeps	**Problem**
1	Memory error
2	Memory error
3	Memory error
4	Memory error
5	CPU error
6	Keyboard controller error
7	CPU error
8	Video card error
9	Faulty BIOS chip
10	CMOS error
11	Cache memory error

REPAIR SERVICE

HOW DO I KNOW WHEN TO TAKE MY COMPUTER TO A REPAIR SERVICE?

There are several factors that determine when you should take your computer to a repair service and which repair service you should use.

DETERMINE IF YOU NEED A REPAIR SERVICE

IDENTIFY THE PROBLEM

When a computer problem occurs, you should troubleshoot the problem yourself. This can help you determine whether the problem is caused by a hardware failure and decide if you need a repair service. For example, if an error message appears when a floppy drive tries to access data on a floppy disk, the problem may be a failing drive or simply a damaged disk.

CONSIDER REPLACING THE COMPONENT

Always consider the cost of repairing a component. Many components, such as floppy drives, are so inexpensive that repairing the component may cost more than replacing it.

You might also consider upgrading a failing component. For example, buying a new, fast CD-ROM drive may cost less than repairing a slow drive.

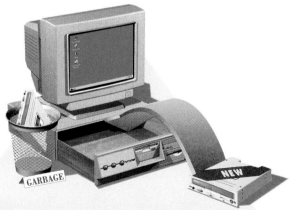

If you choose to replace or upgrade a component, you may want to do the work yourself and avoid using a repair service.

WHEN TO USE A REPAIR SERVICE

ELECTRICAL PROBLEMS

If your computer has severe electrical problems, you should take the computer to a repair service. If you attempt to repair electrical problems in your computer, you may damage the computer or suffer personal injury.

COMPLICATED PROBLEMS

Some problems are the result of several hardware failures occurring at the same time. A problem with multiple causes can be very difficult to troubleshoot and repair. If you are unable to troubleshoot a problem yourself, you may want to use a repair service.

BEFORE GOING TO A REPAIR SERVICE

Once you decide you need a repair service, you should record information about the problem you are experiencing, such as when the problem first happened, how often the problem occurs and what steps the repair service can take to reproduce the problem. It is also helpful to provide a repair service with information about the components and programs installed on the computer. Providing the repair service with as much information as possible can help the repair service fix the problem quickly and efficiently.

TYPES OF REPAIR SERVICES

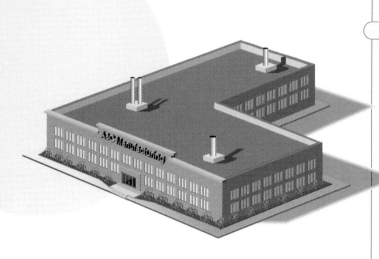

MANUFACTURER

If you have a problem with a component that is under warranty, you may be able to return the component to the manufacturer for replacement or repair. A disadvantage of returning a failing component to the manufacturer is that you may have to pay the shipping costs, which can be expensive.

COMPUTER STORE

Most computer stores have a service department that repairs computers. Prices and quality of work vary greatly between stores. If you purchased your computer from a computer store, you can inquire at that store if they will repair the computer at a reduced cost.

DEDICATED SERVICE COMPANY

Dedicated service companies specialize in repairing computers. Although many dedicated service companies only repair computers for businesses, some will also repair computers for individuals. Dedicated service companies usually charge more than other types of repair services, but they tend to be more skilled.

CHOOSING A REPAIR SERVICE

ESTIMATES

You should use a repair service that will provide a written estimate before the work is performed. After you agree to a price, ask the repair service to contact you if the repair will cost more than the original estimate.

SPEED

You should use a repair service that works quickly, since you will be without the use of your computer while it is being fixed. Try to find out how long it will take a repair service to fix your computer.

RECOMMENDATIONS

You should choose a repair service that has been recommended by someone you trust. Some repair services will give you a list of customers you can contact to verify the quality of the work.

WARRANTY

Many repair services offer warranties, which guarantee their work for a period of time. You should look for at least a 90-day warranty, but a longer warranty is preferable.

WARRANTY SERVICE

IS THERE SERVICE AVAILABLE FOR COMPUTER PRODUCTS COVERED BY A MANUFACTURER'S WARRANTY?

If you have a problem with a computer or component that is covered by a manufacturer's warranty, the manufacturer may repair or replace the product. There are three types of service available—on-site, ship-in and carry-in.

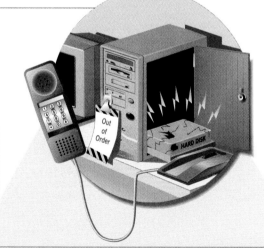

NON-WARRANTY PROBLEMS

You should always troubleshoot a problem yourself to ensure the problem is caused by a product covered by the warranty. If you request warranty service for a problem caused by a product not covered by the warranty, you may have to pay for the time a technician spends investigating the problem.

TELEPHONE TECHNICAL SUPPORT

Most manufacturers offer telephone technical support free of charge for products covered by a warranty. Telephone support is often the first level of technical support available to you when a hardware problem occurs.

Although the technical support is free, you may be on hold a long time. If the call is long-distance and not toll-free, it can be quite expensive.

TYPES OF WARRANTY SERVICE

The warranty determines the type of warranty service you are eligible for, but a telephone technical support representative may determine the type of warranty service you receive.

ON-SITE SERVICE

With on-site service, a technician comes to your home to repair or replace a product. On-site service is usually available when you buy a complete computer system. On-site technicians often carry spare parts and can usually fix problems promptly.

SHIP-IN SERVICE

With ship-in service, you must send a computer or component to the manufacturer to be repaired or replaced. Many manufacturers require that you get an authorization number from a technical support representative before returning a product, and that you ship the product in the original packaging. You may also have to pay the shipping costs, which can be expensive.

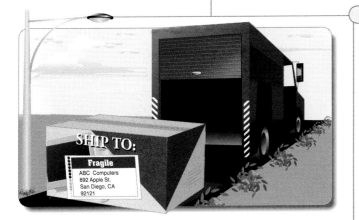

CARRY-IN SERVICE

Carry-in service means that you must take a computer or component to the manufacturer or the store where you purchased it to be repaired or replaced. You will usually have to leave the product for a number of days before it is repaired.

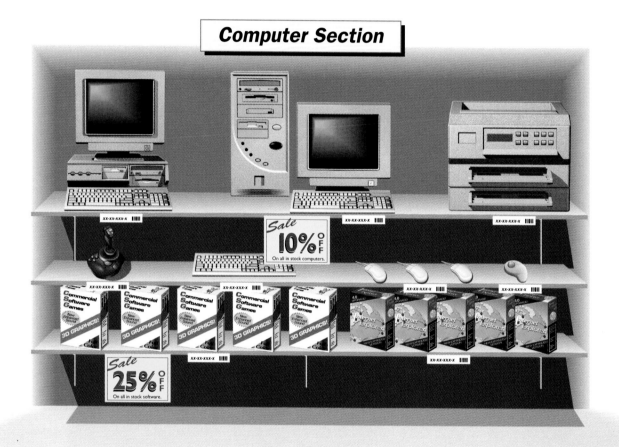

CHAPTER 9

PURCHASE A NEW COMPUTER

Before you purchase a new computer, there are several factors to consider. This chapter compares brand-name and clone computers, outlines specifications and standards and shows you how to build your own computer.

SHOULD I BUY A BRAND-NAME OR CLONE COMPUTER?

There are several factors you should consider when deciding which type of computer is right for you.

CLONE

A clone computer was originally a computer that was not manufactured by IBM but was compatible with the first IBM personal computer. The term clone computer now refers to any computer that is not made by a large computer manufacturer.

Clone computers are becoming more popular because they can contain a variety of components from different manufacturers. This allows you to specify exactly which components you want a computer to contain.

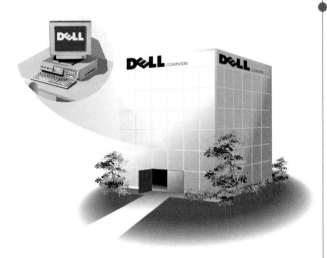

BRAND-NAME

A brand-name computer is a computer made by a large computer manufacturer, such as IBM, Dell or Compaq. Brand-name computers only contain components made or approved by the manufacturer. Most computers that are sold are brand-name computers.

CONSIDERATIONS

COMPATIBILITY

You can upgrade a clone computer more easily than a brand-name computer because a clone computer can support a wider range of components from a variety of different manufacturers. The components in a brand-name computer are often specially designed and expensive to replace, which makes upgrading a brand-name computer more difficult.

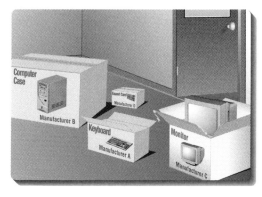

RELIABILITY

Brand-name computers tend to be more reliable than clone computers because the large brand-name computer manufacturers have very rigorous quality control.

COST

Brand-name computers are usually more expensive than clone computers. Although clone computers are less expensive, they are not necessarily of lower quality.

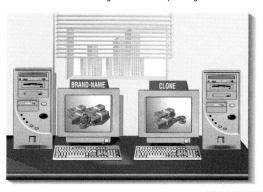

AFTER-SALE SERVICE

Brand-name computers usually come with better after-sale service than clone computers. Brand-name computer manufacturers usually offer an extended warranty, technical support and software support for programs packaged with the computer. This kind of after-sale service is often not available for clone computers.

WHERE TO BUY A COMPUTER

WHERE SHOULD I BUY A COMPUTER?

Where you should buy a computer depends on your budget, whether you want a brand-name or clone computer and the type of after-sale service you require.

You should buy a computer from a business with a good reputation that has been in operation for a number of years.

MANUFACTURERS

Many manufacturers sell computers directly to the public over the telephone or on the Internet. Buying directly from a manufacturer is usually less expensive than buying from a store. You can have the manufacturer build the computer to your specifications, but you are limited to only the components the manufacturer offers. Most manufacturers offer telephone and online technical support services, as well as repair services.

MAIL-ORDER COMPANIES

Most mail-order companies offer computers at discounted prices. Some mail-order companies sell only brand-name computers, while others also offer less expensive clones. Many mail-order companies offer telephone and online technical support services, but you may have to deal directly with the manufacturer for repairs.

You can find advertisements for reputable mail-order companies in most major computer publications.

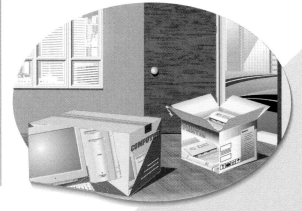

COMPUTER CHAIN STORES

You can find computer chain stores in most major cities. These stores offer a wide selection of brand-name products from popular manufacturers. Chain stores tend to be more expensive than other types of stores, but usually offer good after-sale service, including introductory training classes, technical support and repair services.

INDEPENDENT COMPUTER STORES

Most independent computer stores sell less expensive clone computers and usually do not offer a wide selection of brand-name products. Independent computer stores can be an excellent source of affordable computers, but may not provide adequate after-sale service.

DEPARTMENT STORES

Office supply, electronic and warehouse-type department stores often have a section that sells computers. Most department stores offer brand-name computers at reduced prices, but usually do not have knowledgeable staff to answer your questions or give advice. Some department stores may provide technical support and on-site repair services.

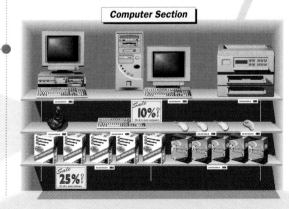

RECOMMENDED COMPUTER SPECIFICATIONS

The options and features you need depend on how you plan to use the computer. There are three main uses of computers—basic, office and home.

WHICH OPTIONS AND FEATURES SHOULD I CHOOSE WHEN BUYING A COMPUTER?

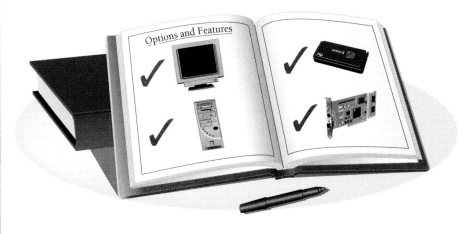

BASIC USE

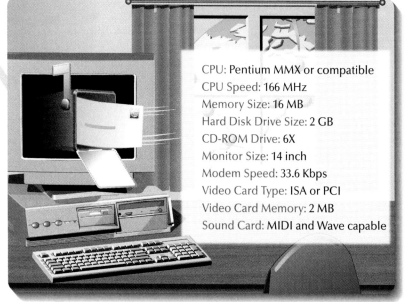

CPU: Pentium MMX or compatible
CPU Speed: 166 MHz
Memory Size: 16 MB
Hard Disk Drive Size: 2 GB
CD-ROM Drive: 6X
Monitor Size: 14 inch
Modem Speed: 33.6 Kbps
Video Card Type: ISA or PCI
Video Card Memory: 2 MB
Sound Card: MIDI and Wave capable

An entry-level, or basic, computer is usually suitable for people new to computing. If you need a computer to perform simple tasks such as exchanging e-mail and browsing the World Wide Web, consider buying a computer with at least the specifications listed to the left.

OFFICE USE

Many office computers do not need to be very powerful, since they are used mostly for word processing and spreadsheet applications. If you need a computer to perform general office tasks, consider buying a computer with at least the specifications listed to the right.

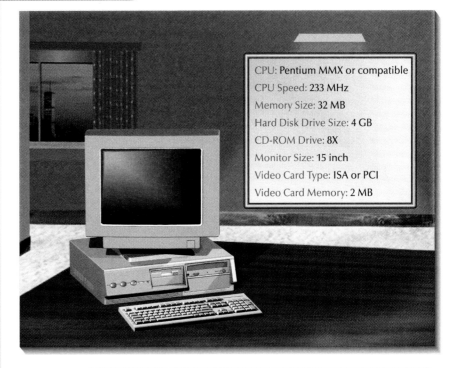

CPU: **Pentium MMX or compatible**

CPU Speed: **233 MHz**

Memory Size: **32 MB**

Hard Disk Drive Size: **4 GB**

CD-ROM Drive: **8X**

Monitor Size: **15 inch**

Video Card Type: **ISA or PCI**

Video Card Memory: **2 MB**

HOME USE

CPU: **Pentium II or equivalent**

CPU Speed: **233 MHz**

Memory Size: **32 MB**

Hard Disk Drive Size: **6 GB**

DVD-ROM Drive: **Second Generation DVD-ROM**

Monitor Size: **15 inch**

Modem Speed: **56 Kbps**

Video Card Type: **PCI or AGP**

Video Card Memory: **4 MB**

Sound Card: **MIDI and Wave capable**

Most home computers need to be powerful because they are often used for playing games and running multimedia applications. When buying a computer for home use, consider buying a computer with at least the specifications listed to the left.

PERSONAL COMPUTER STANDARDS

SHOULD I BE CONCERNED ABOUT STANDARDS WHEN PURCHASING A NEW COMPUTER?

There are several standards that specify the components manufacturers should include in personal computers. By purchasing a computer that meets the most recent standard, you are ensuring that you will be able to use the latest hardware and software on the computer.

COMPATIBILITY

Personal Computer (PC) standards allow hardware and software created by different manufacturers to work together. By following a PC standard, a software manufacturer can be confident that its applications will operate properly on a computer that meets the same PC standard.

DEVELOPMENT

PC standards help define short-term trends in the computer industry, which allows manufacturers to plan the development of new products more effectively. For example, many hardware manufacturers are developing Universal Serial Bus (USB) compatible devices, such as removable storage devices, to take advantage of the USB ports that are built into most new computers.

TYPES OF STANDARDS

MPC3

The Multimedia PC 3 (MPC3) standard was developed by a number of computer companies to specify the components that manufacturers should include in a personal computer that will be used to run multimedia applications. The MPC3 standard is an older standard. All new computers far surpass the MPC3 specifications.

PC 98

The PC 98 standard was developed by Microsoft and Intel. The PC 98 standard specifies the components that manufacturers should include in a computer for home or office use.

PC 99

The PC 99 standard is the successor of PC 98 and is the most recent computer standard from Microsoft and Intel. The PC 99 standard is currently being developed and will come into effect in July of 1999. The PC 99 standard specifies newer components that manufacturers should include in a computer for home or office use, such as a 56 Kbps modem.

PORTABLE COMPUTERS

HOW DOES A PORTABLE COMPUTER DIFFER FROM A DESKTOP COMPUTER?

A portable computer is a small, lightweight computer you can easily transport. A battery or electrical outlet supplies the power for a portable computer.

Because portable computers are much smaller than desktop computers, they require special consideration when being upgraded or repaired.

TYPES OF PORTABLE COMPUTERS

NOTEBOOK

A notebook computer, also called a laptop computer, is the most popular type of portable computer.

You can buy a notebook computer with the same capabilities as a desktop computer, although notebook computers are more expensive.

A notebook computer has a built-in keyboard, pointing device and screen, eliminating the need for cables to connect these devices to the notebook.

DOCKING STATION

You can use a docking station to connect many additional devices to a notebook at once. A docking station can also provide additional features to a notebook computer, such as networking capabilities and a full-size monitor and keyboard.

HANDHELD

A handheld computer is a portable computer that is small enough to carry in your hand. A handheld computer is also called a Personal Digital Assistant (PDA) or pocket computer.

Handheld computers are capable of storing thousands of addresses, appointments and memos. You can use a handheld computer to exchange electronic mail, send and receive faxes and browse the World Wide Web. Some handheld computers also come with word processing and spreadsheet applications.

You can connect a handheld computer to a desktop computer to exchange data between the two computers.

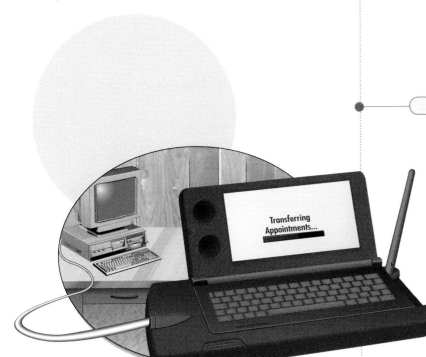

PALM

Palm computers are small handheld computers that are often used as electronic organizers. You can connect a palm computer to a desktop computer to exchange data between the two computers.

Palm computers have many of the same features as handheld computers, but they do not have a keyboard. You use a stylus, or electronic pen, to input data into a palm computer.

SET UP AND TROUBLESHOOT

SETTING UP A PORTABLE COMPUTER

Most notebook computers use the same setup procedures as desktop computers. For example, before you can use a notebook computer, you must install an operating system. You may also need to adjust the computer's settings.

Handheld and palm computers usually have an operating system already installed. Most also have a fixed set of features that do not require you to change any settings.

TROUBLESHOOTING

If you are having problems with a notebook computer, you can use the same diagnostic programs you would use on a desktop computer. A diagnostic program may be able to help you locate and repair problems when a notebook computer malfunctions. Handheld and palm computers often have built-in diagnostic programs. For information on diagnostic programs, see page 186.

If you are having problems with the software you are using on a notebook computer, you can use the same software troubleshooting methods you would use on a desktop computer. For information on troubleshooting software problems, see page 184.

UPGRADE AND REPAIR

UPGRADE

Portable computers have limited upgrade options. Most notebook computers can easily accommodate a larger hard drive or more memory, but it is more difficult to upgrade features such as the screen or processor.

Many components are designed for a specific type of notebook computer. When purchasing new components, make sure you get components that are compatible with your notebook.

Handheld and palm computers can usually have only their memory upgraded.

REPAIR

A portable computer is more difficult to repair than a desktop computer. Compared to desktop computers, portable computers are more likely to have physical problems, such as broken cases and screens, that you cannot repair yourself.

Portable computers also have smaller internal components which are packed into a much smaller space. This can make it difficult to access components in a portable computer. Rather than attempting to repair a portable computer yourself, you should take it to a repair service. For information on repair services, see page 190.

Repair Service

BUILD A COMPUTER

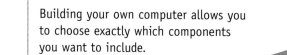

WHY SHOULD I BUILD MY OWN COMPUTER?

Building your own computer allows you to choose exactly which components you want to include.

Although the cost of building your own computer is only slightly less than purchasing a complete computer system, you will have a much better understanding of how a computer works when you finish.

BUILD A COMPUTER

Determine and purchase the computer components and devices you need.

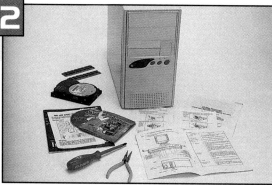

Gather the reference material and computer tools you need. For information on reference material, see page 16. For information on computer tools, see page 6.

Remove the cover from the computer case. For information on computer cases, see page 26.

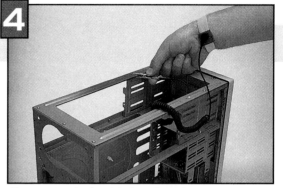

To prevent static electricity from damaging computer components, ground yourself and the computer case. For information on grounding, see page 8.

Install the power supply in the computer case. For information on power supplies, see page 36.

Install the memory modules on the system board. For information on memory, see page 46.

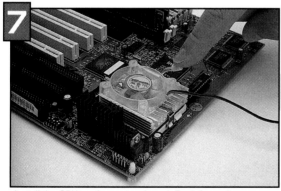

Install the CPU on the system board. For information on CPUs, see page 40.

BUILD A COMPUTER continued

Install the system board in the computer case.
For information on system boards, see page 28.

Install the storage devices, such as a hard drive, floppy drive
or CD-ROM drive, in the computer case. For information on
storage devices, see pages 124 to 151.

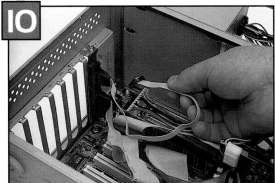

If necessary, install the internal connectors, such as
a parallel or serial port, on the system board. For
information on internal connectors, see page 14.

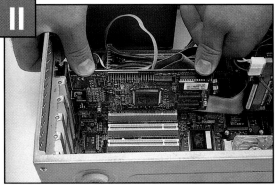

Install the video card on the system board.
For information on video cards, see page 74.

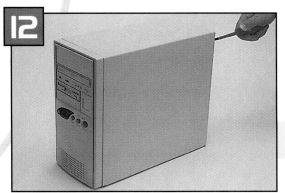

Replace the cover on the computer case.

Connect the monitor, pointing device and keyboard to
the computer. For information on monitors, see page 78.
For information on pointing devices, see page 60. For
information on keyboards, see page 62.

Attach the power cable to the back of the computer and then plug the power cable into an electrical outlet on the wall. Then turn on the computer.

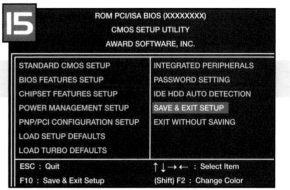

If necessary, adjust the computer's BIOS settings. For information on computer settings, see page 168.

Install the operating system. For information on operating systems, see page 172.

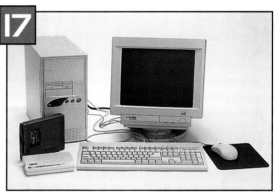

Install any additional devices, such as a modem or sound card.

INDEX

INDEX

OVER 6 MILLION

OTHER 3-D Visual SERIES

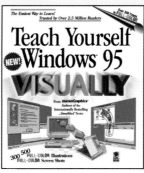

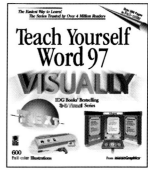

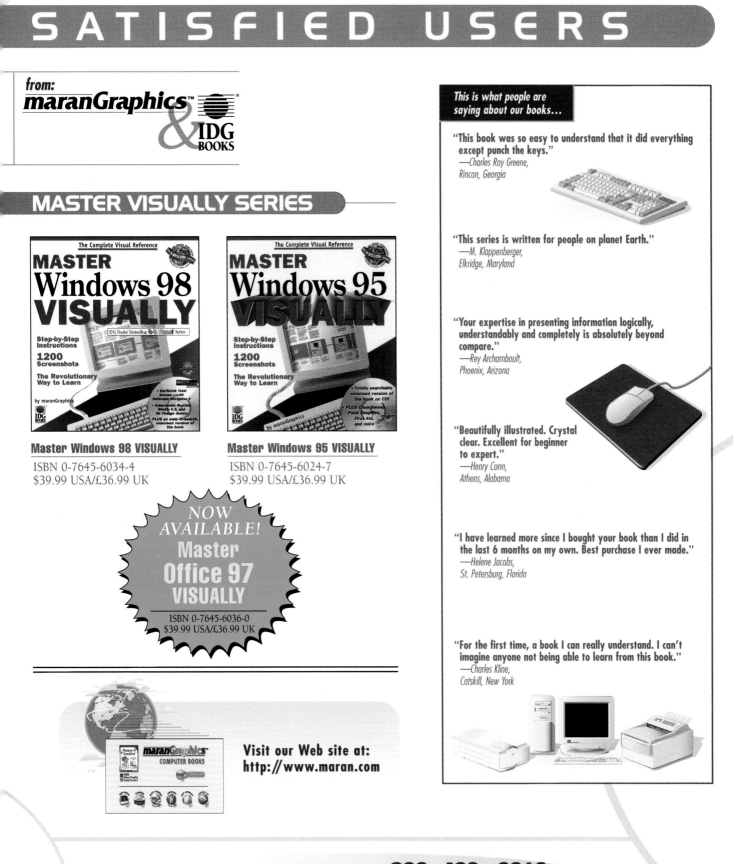

OVER 6 MILLION

OTHER 3-D Visual SERIES

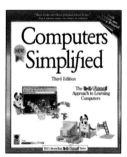

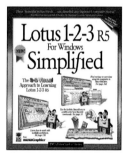

IDG BOOKS®

TRADE & INDIVIDUAL ORDERS

Phone: **(800) 762-2974**
or **(317) 596-5200**
(8 a.m.–6 p.m., CST, weekdays)
FAX : **(800) 550-2747**
or **(317) 596-5692**

EDUCATIONAL ORDERS & DISCOUNTS

Phone: **(800) 434-2086**
(8:30 a.m.–5:00 p.m., CST, weekdays)
FAX : **(317) 596-5499**

CORPORATE ORDERS FOR 3-D VISUAL™ SERIES

Phone: **(800) 469-6616**
(8 a.m.–5 p.m., EST, weekdays)
FAX : **(905) 890-9434**

Qty	ISBN	Title	Price	Total

Shipping & Handling Charges

	Description	First book	Each add'l. book	Total
Domestic	Normal	$4.50	$1.50	$
	Two Day Air	$8.50	$2.50	$
	Overnight	$18.00	$3.00	$
International	Surface	$8.00	$8.00	$
	Airmail	$16.00	$16.00	$
	DHL Air	$17.00	$17.00	$

Subtotal _____

CA residents add
applicable sales tax _____

IN, MA and MD
residents add
5% sales tax _____

IL residents add
6.25% sales tax _____

RI residents add
7% sales tax _____

TX residents add
8.25% sales tax _____

Shipping _____

Total _____

Ship to:

Name _____

Address _____

Company _____

City/State/Zip _____

Daytime Phone _____

Payment: ☐ Check to IDG Books (US Funds Only)
☐ Visa   ☐ Mastercard   ☐ American Express

Card # _____ Exp. _____ Signature _____

maranGraphics™